THE ALMIGHTY WALL

AMERICAN MONOGRAPH SERIES
Editor: Robert A. M. Stern

Bertram Grosvenor Goodhue, Richard Oliver. 1983
The Almighty Wall, The Architecture of Henry Vaughan, William Morgan.
1983

Henry Vaughan, c. 1907.

THE ALMIGHTY WALL

The Architecture of Henry Vaughan

WILLIAM MORGAN

THE ARCHITECTURAL HISTORY FOUNDATION
NEW YORK
THE MIT PRESS, CAMBRIDGE, MASSACHUSETTS
and LONDON, ENGLAND

In Memory Of
ROSEMARY VAUGHAN

William Morgan is Professor of Fine Arts at the University of Louisville.

Library of Congress Cataloging in Publication Data

Morgan, William, 1944–
    The almighty wall.

    (American monograph series)
    Bibliography: p. 188
    1. Vaughan, Henry, 1845–1917.   I. Title.   II. Series:
American monograph series (Architectural History
Foundation (New York, N.Y.)
NA737.V38M67 1982   720'.92'4   82–8766
                                 AACR2
ISBN 0-262-13187-0

Designed by Gilbert Etheredge

CONTENTS

ACKNOWLEDGMENTS

Henry Vaughan left no office records, memoirs, or writings. As a result, the gathering of material for a book on Vaughan and his works was often considerably difficult. Trying to tell the story of one architect's life and influence through his buildings alone has forced the writer to be something of a detective. Many of Vaughan's buildings have no written documentation whatsoever, and thus some of the attributions have been made solely by visual analysis and on-site inspection. The list of works included here must therefore be less than definitive; undoubtedly there are buildings by Vaughan that have eluded me, and a list of his church furnishings and funerary monuments will probably never be complete. Unfortunately, not much more about Vaughan's private life and personality is known now than was known when I began my research in 1968. On the other hand, most of the architect's work survives, and regardless of how frustrating the lack of drawings, papers, articles, and personal memorabilia has been for his biographer, the buildings constitute the record that matters.

Much of the material for this study was supplied by scores of generous people who were willing to share their knowledge, recollections, and even the results of research done on my behalf. This book is thus a collective effort; in fact, it would not have been possible without the help of many scholars, clergy, local historians, and countless correspondents, many of whom I have never met. While the list of everyone who gave assistance would be exceedingly long, I wish to offer my thanks to at least some of them.

Parish priests, cathedral deans, bishops, and other people affiliated with the Episcopal Church gave generously of their time by showing me their churches or by delving into church and diocesan archives: Some of these include Marjorie Raphael, Mother Superior, Society of St. Margaret, Boston; the late Rev. Rowland Cox, Headmaster of the Groton School; Rev. Matthew Warren and William Oates, Rectors of St. Paul's School; Rev. William Kibitz, Rector-Emeritus, and Rev. David Boulton, Rector of Christ Church, New Haven, Connecticut; Rev. Robert Brown, Rector of St. Peter's Church, Ripon, Wisconsin, and historian of the Diocese of Fond du Lac; Rev. Donald E. Bitsberger, Rector of the Church of the Redeemer, Chestnut Hill, Massachusetts; Rev. Allen Joslin, Rector-Emeritus, Christ Church, Swansea, Massachusetts; and Rev. Frank Knight, Rector of the Church of the Mediator, Bronx, New York. Richard T. Feller, Clerk of the Works of Washington Cathedral, has been a friend and adviser since the inception of my work on Vaughan.

I am grateful for the support and guidance of the Architectural History Foundation, and to architect and teacher Robert A. M. Stern who brought my previous writing on Vaughan to the Foundation's attention. Ned Pratt researched St. Timothy's Church in Concord, New Hampshire, and first introduced me to St. Paul's School, while Douglas Stern, Historic Preservation Officer of the City of Evansville, has made many helpful suggestions. The late Lloyd Hendrick provided invaluable assistance in sharing his recollections of his tenure in Henry Vaughan's office.

Robert De Lage of Attleboro, Massachusetts, worked tirelessly to uncover information regarding Vaughan's association with Edward F. Searles; without his interest and enthusiasm, that aspect of Vaughan's career would certainly be less well known. Similarly, Jim Lewis of Pasadena, California, contributed immeasurably to this book through his photographs and by his careful printing of others. That we know so much of the Boston Gothicists is due to the work of Douglass Shand Tucci, whose work on Ralph Adams Cram has provided a model of scholarship for the period, and who argued for the need for a proper study of Vaughan. John Coolidge of Harvard discussed the text on many occasions during his tenure as the F. L. Morgan Professor of Architectural Design at the University of Louisville, and his critical comments and perceptive observations have strengthened this book.

In England, research on Vaughan has been assisted by a number of people, among them Bodley's biographer, David Verey; Hermione Waterfield of Christie's; and Major Elliott Viney, Buckinghamshire's greatest living treasure. The Vaughan story is also part of the heritage of a family who welcomed me as one of their own. Henry Vaughan's nephew and godson, the late A. Ronald Vaughan, his nephew Patrick Brims of Oxford, and especially Mr. Vaughan's daughters Yvonne and Rosemary of Colyton, Devon, supplied both information and continual encouragement. Rosemary's untimely death in 1980 was the catalyst for this attempt to record Henry Vaughan's legacy.

Carolyn, Whitney, Jamey, Joel, and Lindsay provided the happy environment in which this book was written.

FOREWORD

The career of Henry Vaughan—leading figure of the Boston Gothicists, as the author calls him—rushes the observer headlong into confrontation with the idea of progress in art. In the grand scheme of things, the emphasis on progress—in the sense of typological and stylistic innovation—is a relatively recent phenomenon. It was the open-armed acclaim with which the twentieth century greeted modernism that for some time resulted in an equally fervent repudiation of everything that had preceded it. Novelty came to be valued for its own sake regardless of the aesthetic and environmental consequences.

Given this attitude, what was to be made of the many fine buildings which are neither revolutionary nor even inventive? The contribution made by such architecture is a major one, and the master builders of that long and honorable tradition married rediscovery, study, and appreciation. And yet the architects of these buildings have been overlooked.

It could be argued that within the Gothic Revival Vaughan played the role of an innovator in his return to an earlier and purer style than that of his more worldly contemporaries. But the present study addresses his advance—the advance toward complete mastery within an established tradition—rather than his progress toward something new. Vaughan was a master of the neo-Gothic: his work represents a landmark of the late and most dramatic phase of this style. His freshness of interpretation and his extraordinarily ever-growing command of a chosen idiom provide an instructive model for us today. As a master, as a model, and as a memory, Henry Vaughan is recalled in the following pages.

Robert A. M. Stern

THE ALMIGHTY WALL

1. St. John's Chapel, Groton School, Groton, Massachusetts, 1899–1900.

INTRODUCTION

There was considerable dispute, of course, as to the style of architecture to be used. Strong opinion favored either brick or "the New England meeting house," but the final decision was for Gothic. It was a good decision, for although the Chapel differed from the other buildings, perhaps a chapel should differ, and this chapel dominates not only the entire school grounds but the whole countryside. It is the first thing a boy sees as he comes to the school; the last as he leaves. It reaches at heaven, but it is substantial, simple, and spacious on the earth.

Peabody of Groton

ST. JOHN'S Chapel at Groton School (Fig. 1) is one of Henry Vaughan's masterpieces. As such, it is one of the major monuments in the history of Gothic Revival architecture in America.

Some years before I embarked on a career in architectural history, the Groton Chapel provided me with a memorable architectural experience. As a teenager visiting in a nearby town, I was taken to a Christmas service at this Massachusetts preparatory school. Few religious celebrations caught my imagination and moved me as did that festival of carols and lessons, and I long remembered the sound of the boys' choir and the flickering candlelight beneath the dark timber ceiling (Fig. 2). The architect who had created such a setting was, to my mind, a genius.

Later, when I visited Vaughan's other great chapel at St. Paul's School in Concord, New Hampshire (Fig. 3), I was convinced that Henry Vaughan was an architect worthy of both study and recognition. And it was largely because so little had been written about the creator of these two Gothic Revival landmarks that I decided to write my doctoral dissertation on this forgotten Anglo-American architect.

I was baptized in Ralph Adams Cram's Princeton University Chapel, and I grew up among the Gothic splendors of that idyllic "Oxford in America" which Cram and other architects had fashioned in New Jersey. So it is perhaps appropriate that I should have been drawn to the Gothic Revival. However, I was trained by those who had fought the battle for modern architecture, and I was taught that the work of Vaughan and

1

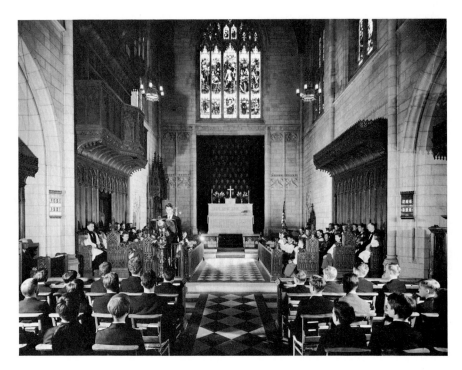

2. Groton Chapel, interior.

Cram and other revivalist architects was not supposed to be admired, much less praised. Generally, my teachers used the term "eclecticism" as if it were some sort of disease and regarded nonhistoricist architects such as Louis Sullivan, Frank Lloyd Wright, and Walter Gropius as the apostles of "Truth." An historian simply did not appreciate a building like the Groton Chapel, especially because its east and west windows were, according to John Coolidge, "careful reproductions of the Parish Church at Edington in Wiltshire,"[1] and the tower was based on a West Country example, like the one at Ilminster in Somerset.[2]

But it is pointless to make an apology for Vaughan as a non-"form-follows-function" modernist, for his buildings stand for a philosophy beyond their eclectic sources. The many parish churches, scholastic works, and cathedral designs speak eloquently, if modestly, of a renascent Episcopal Church and a religious spirit that are just as much a part of the late nineteenth-century architectural landscape as Sullivan's skyscrapers. Henry Vaughan's role in the Gothic Revival was much like that of Charles McKim in the revival of neoclassicism.[3]

2

Henry Vaughan's arrival on the American architectural scene in 1881 marked a first step in the resuscitation of the Gothic Revival, a style that had been unable to withstand the onslaught of the tremendously vital Romanesque of Henry Hobson Richardson. But Vaughan was more than a transitional figure who bridged the gap between the Victorian Gothic Revival of the 1860s and 1870s (represented by architects like Richard M. Upjohn, Henry M. Congdon, and Charles C. Haight) and its closing, Edwardian phase which flourished until the late 1920s. This Modern Gothic incorporated two distinct stylistic tendencies; one leans toward a more archaeologically strict expression, the other toward a more synthetic and interpretive approach to historic precedents. Vaughan was the daystar of the more archaeological approach, as well as one of its finer exponents.[4]

Although little is known of Vaughan's education and practice in England prior to his immigration to America, it is clear that his preparation in the Gothic tradition of mid-Victorian Britain set him apart from his American colleagues. Although David B. Emerson, a Boston contem-

3. Chapel of St. Peter and St. Paul, St. Paul's School, Concord, New Hampshire, 1886–1894.

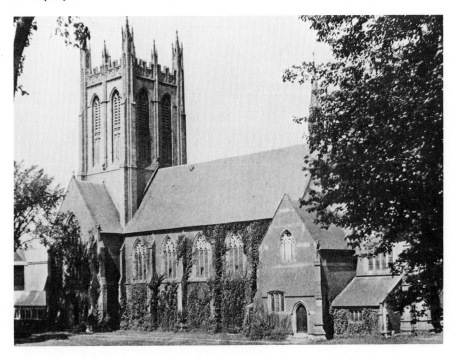

3

porary of Vaughan's, suggested that he may have been apprenticed to either of the leading Gothicists, Sir George Gilbert Scott or George Edmund Street, it is more likely that he received his training with George Frederick Bodley, the architect for whom he served as head draftsman for a number of years.[5] What is important is that Vaughan was not only trained in, but was also familiar with, the work of the leading practitioners of the Gothic Revival in England. Very few Gothic Revival architects in America possessed the background and sophistication of the 36-year-old Vaughan at the time of his arrival in this country. Vaughan's reasons for forsaking England for the United States remain obscure. Without documentary evidence, it would be hard to state definitely that Vaughan really came with the purpose of "interpreting Gothic architecture to America," but there seems little doubt that he was qualified to design much more historically accurate Gothic architecture than had been seen in America.[6]

For Cram, the major proponent of the Gothic style, such academic purity was found primarily in the work of the nineteenth-century English Gothicists, to whom he acknowledged his debt:

When in the course of time, I had an office of my own and felt the impulse to build churches, it was the elder group of these English masters to which I turned for leadership and guidance, with Vaughan, of course, as the local mentor. There could have been no better and I am grateful to them. Behind all lay the great work of the Catholic Middle Ages . . . but the great English builders gave the inspiration towards making Gothic alive again, and showed how this was to be done.[7]

The inspiration to which Cram referred was not merely nationalistic, but—more important—religious. Thus another characteristic of the late Gothic Revival was its identification with the Anglican Communion, a denomination that experienced regeneration in the nineteenth century, both in England and America. As a prolific writer and articulate spokesman of Gothic for America, Cram argued that English Gothic architecture of the fourteenth century—before Henry VIII's break with Rome and prior to the introduction of Renaissance styles—was the natural starting point for the development of an American ecclesiastical architecture. Anglo-American architecture should, in short, purge itself of later, more Protestant forms.

Cram's somewhat romantic architectural and religious philosophy was an American manifestation of the English High Church movement that had developed during the nineteenth century, particularly at Oxford and Cambridge universities. Led by such groups as the Cambridge Camden Society (or the Ecclesiologists), this revitalization sought to incorporate church design with liturgical reform and directly affected church building in America as well as in England. In fact, Ecclesiology was the single most important influence on the development of the Gothic Revival in America, particularly in its early stages.[8]

The Ecclesiologists, through their journal of the same name, offered ideal church plans that conformed with their thoughts on what an Anglican house of worship should be. They also praised those architects who lived up to their expectations, while they attacked designs which they found wanting. A favorable review in *The Ecclesiologist* could mean more commissions; an unfavorable one could seriously hinder a church builder's career. Whether or not such power was always wielded fairly, these arbiters of ecclesiastical design found much of their material (and not a little of their moral stance) in the polemical treatises of Augustus Welby Northmore Pugin published in the 1840s. Although the Anglican reformers could not forgive Pugin for his conversion to Roman Catholicism, they found his arguments about the need to recover the architectural and ecclesiastical forms of the 1440s irresistible. In this sense, both Bodley and Vaughan were Puginians. Similarly, the ideas of Pugin achieved greater currency through their advocacy by John Ruskin, the most influential architectural critic of his, or perhaps any, age. Ruskin's writings had wide popular appeal, and through them, the philosophy espoused by Pugin and the Ecclesiologists became an accepted part of Victorian culture.

Vaughan's buildings clearly indicate that he was not only familiar with the High Church movement, but was a sympathetic member of it. Cram called Vaughan "the apostle of the new dispensation," heir to the "steady and noble work of Bodley and Garner and Sedding," men who had "suppressed" Victorian Gothic and restored continuity with the original movement begun by Pugin.[9] American architects like Richard Upjohn, John Notman, and James Renwick served the High Church cause in the 1840s and 1850s, but by the 1870s and 1880s the vision of Pugin and the Ecclesiologists had been clouded by non-English sources from Venice and elsewhere and by the employment of Gothic for nonecclesiastical purposes. While at Trinity Church in Boston, Richardson provided almost an antidote to the picturesque excesses of Victorian Gothic—such as Cummings & Sears's 1874 Byzantine-Venetian New Old South Church opposite Copley Square from Trinity (Fig. 4). Vaughan's entry into this architectural arena just at the peak of Richardson's career marked the beginning of a movement that was to develop as a new phase of the

4. Cummings & Sears, New Old South Church, Boston, 1874–1875.

Gothic Revival. In fact, one Boston colleague, David Emerson, categorically stated that

Gothic architecture has never been a living reality until Henry Vaughan began his work, which may have been equaled but will never be surpassed. To make the assertion that his influence and the inspiration given by his work have made possible the very high class of Gothic work done by his contemporaries is not making too great a claim for him.[10]

Thus, the Chapel for the Sisters of Saint Margaret of 1881 on Louisburg Square in Boston is a pivotal work for several reasons, not least of all that it was the first work by Vaughan in this country.[11] Not only were Episcopal female orders practically unknown at this time,[12] but this small private chapel incorporated some then-uncommon architectural elements. Only the chapel's west wall, with a single window, faces Pinckney Street and is visible to the passerby. This Decorated window, and particularly the proportional relationship of window to wall, is immediately English, calling to mind the work of architects like Pugin and Bodley.

6

The major elements of the chapel's interior (Fig. 5)—the wood-trussed barrel vault, the placement of the seats "in choir," the ornate rood screen, and the richness of the furnishings—are Vaughan hallmarks that appeared in subsequent work (the altar and the reredos were designed by Vaughan but were executed by Robert Casson in 1922). Some of these features had been seen in America before, but their combination was rare even in the more ecclesiological of American churches before this time.

Considering Vaughan's age and training, it is not surprising that his first American commission was so thoroughly English. More remarkable is the fact that for the next three and a half decades Vaughan's designs seemed almost totally unaffected by the New World, nor was his work perceptibly influenced by any American practitioners. Henry Vaughan was, in short, an English architect who happened to work in America.

5. St. Margaret's Chapel, Boston, 1882–1883, interior.

Vaughan contributed to American architecture through the introduction of ecclesiastical and educational architecture based on proper medieval models. Because of the new styles he brought to America, Vaughan was part of the late phase of nineteenth-century Romanticism which is popularly known as the "Gilded Age." The desire of Cram and the Boston Gothicists for more correct English Gothic buildings was another facet of America at the turn of the century, when a whole panoply of past styles was used, as if they offered a sense of stability while the country took its first hesitant steps as a world power. When Vaughan arrived in America, Chester Arthur was president, and although Presidents Cleveland, Harrison, and McKinley led the country during much of his career, it was the administrations of Theodore Roosevelt and Woodrow Wilson that most accurately reflected the cultural spirit of which Vaughan's work was a part. While Roosevelt curbed the abuses of the Robber Barons, his vision and policies of America as an imperial democracy were based on the British model. His pro-British sentiments were further expressed in his anti-isolationist stance during the First World War. Woodrow Wilson, too, was a great Anglophile—he was responsible for the transformation of the Princeton University campus into a New World recreation of Oxford and Cambridge—and, although a Presbyterian, Wilson was buried in Washington Cathedral, that supreme monument of Episcopalianism in America. Vaughan's thoroughly English architecture—school chapels, half-timber village churches, and even castles—had the same sort of appeal as the French chateaux and Renaissance palazzi of the period. The English-inspired styles especially offered legitimacy in their reassurance of a common heritage—language, religion, customs—with the mother country.

Although it is not known precisely why Vaughan chose to leave England, it is very likely that he acted from a genuine missionary impulse to bring English Gothic to the American branch of the Church of England.[13] Whatever the reasons for his decision, there were Americans who were receptive to Vaughan's particular architectural preferences. His English stylistic repertory was never significantly modified during his thirty-six years in America. In fact, there is no reason to suppose that he would not have produced virtually the same type of designs had he stayed in England. But while the basic elements of most of these styles had appeared in America before, Vaughan was one of the first to revive the half-timbering and the Elizabethan-Jacobean modes that became popular in America in the early twentieth century.

During his practice in America, Vaughan produced dozens of churches and school buildings, as well as plans for one of the largest ecclesiastical structures of this century, the National Cathedral in Washington. Working in a small office in Boston, Vaughan designed primarily churches and academic structures, including the chapels for Groton and St. Paul's schools, as well as three chapels for the Cathedral of St. John the Divine in New York. Some, like the chapel for St. Paul's, were influential in their own right. But almost all of Vaughan's buildings were known for their consistently high quality and for the architect's thoroughness and attention to detail—the direct result of Vaughan's training with Bodley during the flowering of the Arts and Crafts Movement. In New England, at least, a Vaughan church was the standard by which other churches were measured.

Why then is such an architect who was revered and respected by his profession in his own lifetime so forgotten today?[14] Doubtless one answer is provided by the vagaries of architectural taste. Happily, in the 1970s, Cram and his generation of late Gothicists were rediscovered and their careers began to be reassessed.[15] In fact, Victorian architecture—so long out of favor—has now achieved a position of respectability and admiration. Acceptance of the intrinsic merit of nonmodernist, late nineteenth- and early twentieth-century architecture has even filtered down to the popular press, as, for example, in the following statement from the *New York Times*:

. . . the professional leaders of that age, architects like McKim, Mead & White, Cass Gilbert, Burnham & Root, were designing buildings that shaped their time as much as did, say, the work of more innovative architects like Frank Lloyd Wright.[16]

But probably the greatest single reason for Vaughan's obscurity is the man himself. One of his assistants, George Barton, remembers Vaughan as solitary, apparently "lonesome in the extreme," having come to this country as a stranger without friends, influence, or money.[17] Vaughan avoided publicity as strenuously as the gregarious and extroverted Cram sought it. As Clarence Blackall, a Boston architect, recalled shortly after Vaughan's death:

Mr. Vaughan's life has been almost a mystery to the present generation of architects. He was an influence rather than a personality to the younger men and a personality which was felt rather than by the actual work he accomplished . . . modest to the last degree about his own achievements, mingling rarely

9

with his fellow architects, never accepting a commission unless he could personally attend to every detail thereof, his whole life wrapped up in the art of his profession . . . a man who exerted a surprising influence in an almost absolutely unseen manner. [18]

Vaughan, like the anonymous medieval mason, believed that his buildings would live long after his name was forgotten.

Because of Vaughan's extremely self-effacing character, there is a dearth of documentary material about him and his work. Since he never married, there was no devoted wife or family, or really even friends, to collect, publish, and pass on his story to future generations. Even while Vaughan was working on the National Cathedral, his office had neither telephone, typewriter, nor secretary—letters and specifications were personally written in long hand—and no office records survive. Although a few churches do have some original drawings, far too few Vaughan buildings have anything approaching complete documentation. [19]

With so few written records upon which to draw, the primary sources for a study of Henry Vaughan must be the buildings themselves. Vaughan did not care whether these suggested something of the man who designed them. Content to remain an unknown craftsman, Vaughan eschewed personal glory and wished only to serve his God through his art. His legacy, however, constitutes a remarkably rich chapter in the history of American architecture.

1

A SOLITARY LIFE

His life was apparently lonesome in the extreme. From his rooms to his office, from his office to Marston's restaurant and back again, was practically his entire life. According to American standards it was dull, uninteresting, dreary. It was, however, full of a sweetness and richness which, while un-American, was still very good for America.

George Edward Barton

HENRY VAUGHAN, the seventh and youngest child of Thomas Barnes Vaughan and Septima Puella (Bond) Vaughan, was born January 17, 1845, in Bebbington, Rockferry, Cheshire, and christened in St. Peter's Church there on May 25 of the same year.[1] While Henry was still a child, his father moved the family to Dollar in Clackmannanshire, Scotland, supposedly so that his children— or at least his sons— could be educated at Dollar Academy. When Henry was sixteen, his father, who had a heart condition, was accidentally poisoned. However, Henry undoubtedly completed his secondary education at Dollar, and the bronze medal he received in 1863—"Local prize for success in Art awarded by the Department of Science and Art"—was probably a graduation award.[2]

Biographical material about Vaughan's early life is virtually nonexistent, but he probably began an apprenticeship in an architect's office at this time. One family member, Rosemary Vaughan, noted that Henry was remembered as "the most brilliant student of the Royal Institute of British Architects."[3] Vaughan was also skilled in other arts. A small still life (Fig. 6) by him exists; the family believes that it is the only painting he did, but it is sufficiently accomplished to suggest that he did other pictures. Yvonne Vaughan (granddaughter of Vaughan's brother William) owns a straight-backed side chair in a simplified Chippendale style which Vaughan designed and probably made. Vaughan's brother William was a civil and marine engineer who built a number of

6. Still life, oil painting by Henry Vaughan.

bridges, so some family inclination toward the professions associated with construction can be assumed.[4]

Since so much of Vaughan's work bears the imprint of George Frederick Bodley's personal interpretation of English Gothic, much of his training was undoubtedly in Bodley's office. Vaughan later referred to Bodley as his "dear old Master" and "the most lovable man I have ever known." He wrote in 1907 that he had "known Mr. Bodley for nearly forty years," thus setting the beginning of their association at about 1867, when Vaughan was twenty-two.[5] If Vaughan apprenticed with Scott or with another architect, it would have been during the few years before 1867 for which no records remain.

George Frederick Bodley (1827–1907, Fig. 7), the son of a Brighton physician, became at the age of eighteen Sir George Gilbert Scott's first pupil, serving the customary five-year apprenticeship and living in his master's house.[6] Scott churned out so many buildings and trained so many younger architects that he might more accurately be thought of as presiding over a kind of design factory. If Vaughan had also apprenticed with Scott, Bodley would have quickly dispelled the effects of Scott's almost mechanical approach and enlisted Vaughan in the revolt against the rigid conventions of an English Gothic called by Edward Warren, an apprentice of Bodley, "revived, but not revivified."[7] But if the references to Vaughan's having been a student of Scott's cannot be totally ignored, the majority of sources seem to agree that he trained under Bodley.[8]

Thus, Vaughan began his professional association with Bodley around 1867 and served as head draftsman of the firm of Bodley & Garner until he left for Boston in 1881.[9] Although it is difficult to determine exactly which buildings Vaughan may have helped to design, as head draftsman

7. George Frederick Bodley.

we can assume that he did drawings for most of them. During this time the firm received some of its most important commissions: St. Augustine's Church, Pendlebury (1870–1874, Fig. 8); the Church of the Holy Angels at Hoar Cross (1872–1876, Fig. 9); and St. Michael's, Camden Town, London (1876–1881), as well as the Master's House, University College, Oxford (1876–1879), and St. Swithun's Quadrangle, Magdalen College (also at Oxford and begun 1880). The spirit, character, and, not least of all, details of these works found further expression later in Vaughan's own buildings.

One of Bodley's earliest churches, St. Michael's, Brighton (1858–1862), was in a somewhat French, High Victorian manner.[10] After that church he limited himself to English models, primarily fourteenth-century Gothic (or Decorated), which he considered "the most beautiful architecture the world has ever known."[11] Bodley & Garner also drew from the

8. Bodley & Garner, St. Augustine's Church, Pendlebury, Manchester, 1870–1874.

9. *Bodley & Garner, Church of the Holy Angels,*
Hoar Cross, Staffordshire, 1872–1876, exterior.

whole range of English Gothic styles, including Tudor, Elizabethan, and
Stuart variants.

Bodley's churches represented a break from the stock plans and
moldings used by architects of Scott's generation and marked a return to
the purer ecclesiological tenets espoused by Pugin. The hallmarks of
Bodley's work are refinement, sensibility, and an "avoidance of extravagance of Manner"; as a result he "wielded greater influence on church

15

architecture after the death of Street than any other architect during the last years of the nineteenth and beginning of the twentieth centuries."[12] Although Bodley's plans are not necessarily ecclesiological—that is, following the strictures laid down by the Cambridge Camden Society in the 1840s and 1850s—roods, screens, stations of the cross, and other Anglo-Catholic features were employed; brick was often used for the walls rather than stone, and, unlike French-inspired Gothic, wood trussing or a cradle roof was preferred to masonry vaulting.

The quality that really set a Bodley church apart, however, was the total harmony and richness of its decoration, all of it either designed by, or at least overseen by, the architect himself. Leaving nothing to the whim of the decorator or cabinetmaker, Bodley designed the furniture, decoration, and all the many church accessories, including altar vessels and vestments, with "infinite care" (as Vaughan reported).[13] Patterned wall painting, for example, was one of the medieval decorative practices that Bodley helped to revive. In other areas he wisely relied on the talents of the leading artisans of the day, especially the Pre-Raphaelite Brotherhood. In one church alone (St. Martin's, Scarborough, consecrated 1862) Bodley employed Edward Burne-Jones, William Morris, Spencer Stanhope, Philip Webb, Ford Madox Brown, and Dante Gabriel Rossetti.[14] For his stained glass (in addition to Morris and Burne-Jones) Bodley relied on Charles Eamer Kempe (Fig. 10), who worked in the Pre-Raphaelite manner.[15] Reflecting the philosophy of the Arts and Crafts Movement, Bodley's churches show a delight in the polychromy that resulted from the juxtaposition of stone and wood, glass, gilding, and painting. Only by his meticulousness was Bodley able to avoid what in other hands would have been overstatement and confusion.[16] As Edward Warren would later note:

No detail has been overlooked, the finish is careful and minute. It is safe to say that in the enthusiastic, scholarly and patient completion of every accessory, ceremonial or decorative, of a church interior Messrs. Bodley and Garner stood in the early "seventies" absolutely alone.[17]

Much of what has been said of Bodley's work could equally well be said of Vaughan's, for, like his master, Vaughan's approach to design encompassed all of the lesser details of a building.[18] There can be little doubt that Bodley was the most important influence in Vaughan's career, a conclusion that Vaughan's eulogy of the elder man confirms.[19] Bodley was one of Vaughan's few close friends, and the two were not dissimilar

16

10. *Henry Vaughan,*
John William Lisle,
and Charles Eamer Kempe,
Lindfield, Sussex, 1904.

in manner and temperament. Vaughan shared his mentor's belief both in the church and in English Gothic architecture, and, like his disciple, Bodley had a retiring nature and avoided publicity. It has been said that no architect of his eminence in England was so little known.[20]

Perhaps Bodley was responsible for Vaughan's decision to remain in America after completing St. Margaret's chapel. Vaughan recalled that Bodley talked

. . . much about America, and his hope and belief that new world Gothic architecture would take deep root, and flourish as it had done only in England in the middle ages.[21]

Vaughan may also have been encouraged to come to this country by the young American architect Halsey Wood, who apprenticed with Bodley & Garner for about a year in 1879.[22] Wood undoubtedly told Vaughan of the need for architects of the Anglican persuasion in America, and the two men remained on friendly terms.[23] Cram stated that Vaughan came to the United States specifically to do the chapel for the Sisters of St. Margaret,[24] but this does not explain why he remained in Boston. It is, however, more than coincidental that Vaughan's first commission was for this order.

The Society of St. Margaret was founded in 1855 by the Tractarian divine John Mason Neale. In 1871 a part of the St. Margaret sisterhood came to Boston and took charge of Children's Hospital. The Society was not under the direction of the diocese of Massachusetts but was instead associated with the Society of St. John the Evangelist (known as the Cowley Fathers); these English orders remained separate and unknown to the Boston community at large. As they looked to England for guidance in matters religious and artistic, it is hardly surprising that St. Margaret's sought a sympathetic architect there.[25] Not only did Vaughan come to America to work for St. Margaret's, but he worshipped with the

11. St. Andrew's Church, Newcastle, Maine, 1883.

Cowley Fathers at St. John the Evangelist on Bowdoin Street.[26] He quickly became the favored designer not only for the few Anglican orders in late nineteenth-century America but for New England's small High Church coterie.

Vaughan's next job after St. Margaret's was for chancel furniture—rood screen, choir stalls, pulpit, credence table, altar, and reredos—for St. Stephen's Church in Providence, Rhode Island, an 1860 work by Richard Upjohn.[27] This important early commission suggests the direction Vaughan's career was going to take—as an architect who could satisfy High Church parishes in their striving for aesthetic independence in a region that had been traditionally hostile to Anglicanism. Vaughan's work at St. Stephen's was cited for its "conspicuous artistic merit" and for its "unusual ecclesiological correctness."[28]

The cabinetwork for St. Stephen's was done by the firm of Irving & Casson and the stone carving by Evans & Tombs. The principals of these companies, Robert Casson and John Evans, were among the few close friends that Vaughan had, and both were, like him, British immigrants.

Between the St. Margaret's commission and that for St. Andrew's Church in Newcastle, Maine, of 1883 (Fig. 11), Vaughan could hardly have had a great deal of work. As Barton recalls, "he apparently buried himself in two little rooms over the Criminal Investigation Department in Pemberton Square. . . . He made no effort to get work."[29] Curiously, Vaughan appears in some group photographs of Richardson's assistants taken around 1886 (Fig. 12). One can only guess what Vaughan was doing in Richardson's office, but it supports the statement made by one of Vaughan's draftsmen, Lloyd Hendrick, that young designers moved rather freely between architectural firms.

Hendrick, a 1912 graduate of Harvard, worked for Vaughan in 1916 and 1917 and recounted his experiences with Vaughan and the workings of his office.[30] Vaughan was occupied with the designs for the National Cathedral in Washington, a commission that was awarded to Bodley and Vaughan in 1907. Hendrick related that the office, even when engaged in such a major project, included only Vaughan, three draftsmen, and an office boy. Everything was done in a very "old time way." Vaughan regarded the telephone as an intrusion and one suspects that a female secretary would have been equally unwelcome (occasionally the head draftsman typed out a letter with one finger, and sometimes Mrs. Hendrick typed specifications at home). Vaughan roughed out all of the drawings for Washington, which were then turned over to an assistant whose work Vaughan later critiqued.

19

Hendrick remembered Vaughan as a "real loner" and a "distant man" who kept to himself in a private office, where he spent most of his time drawing. Vaughan had short red hair, a neatly trimmed full beard, and piercing steel-blue eyes. He was, Hendrick recalled, "friendly, but not outgoing." He never talked about his private life or mentioned his family; Robert Casson, the cabinetmaker, was his only intimate friend. Vaughan always returned to the office at night, although he never allowed his employees to do so. This was because Vaughan did not want his

12. *Henry Hobson Richardson's assistants in Richardson's office, c. 1886 (Vaughan is seated, second from the left).*

draftsmen to disturb the mice that came to feed on the crumbs of a roll that he brought back from his supper. The sparrows in Pemberton Square came to Vaughan's window to be fed, and as an animal lover he condemned all forms of hunting.

Vaughan died suddenly and unexpectedly of lung cancer on June 30, 1917, at the home of Robert Casson in suburban Newton Center. A service was held at Trinity Church in Newton Center on July 3, and his body was taken to Forest Hills cemetery in Boston until its removal to

21

Washington Cathedral that October.[31] Although his will was not officially recorded, Vaughan left handsome bequests to his four nieces and nephews of £3,000 apiece, with the residue going to the "Boston family with whom he had been living."[32]

While Vaughan's personal life may have indeed been dreary and uninteresting, he apparently felt that his work was sufficient justification for such a stern, monkish existence. In David Emerson's words,

True artist that he was, he cared little whether it was known or not, so long as it was well done and he was as conscientious and painstaking in designing a hundred dollar gravestone to go in a country churchyard, as in the design of a city church that would be seen by all.[33]

The Boston Society of Architects (of which Vaughan was a founding member, but never a participant) eulogized:

We knew Mr. Vaughan as typifying the best and purest expression of English Gothic architecture which this country has seen. He was never at fault for artistic expression, never in doubt as to what was the right thing to do and absolutely refused to do anything but what his architectural conscience told him was right. We have only too few of this sort in the profession. Uncompromising to the last degree, but doing his work with such care and with such wonderful results that though he worked in a style in which few architects ever cared to attempt and only a very few ever mastered, his influence on the work of the profession was very strong.[34]

2

THE PARISH CHURCHES

Generations of the faithful must have worshipped here, we feel, and yet the church is but a few years built. . . . Happy is the man who can so design and build as to inspire men for centuries. Saturated with the finest traditions of English Gothic, humble-minded, and of the strictest artistic integrity, Henry Vaughan never aimed to be original. His joy was to express in its purest architectural form the aspirations of the Anglo-Saxon race as to create the atmosphere and spirit of worship.

William Lawrence, *Church Militant*, October 1917

WITH THE building of his first church, St. Andrew's in Newcastle, Maine, Henry Vaughan set the pattern for the many parish churches that he created during his career. Like St. Andrew's, they were evocations of the English medieval church-building tradition. Vaughan's parish churches provided a feeling of place and established a sense of identity that was synonymous with the rejuvenation of the Church of England's American counterpart, the Episcopal Church.

Overlooking the Damariscotta River in the small coastal village of Newcastle, St. Andrew's (Fig. 11), one of Vaughan's most thoroughly satisfying designs, was donated and endowed by Captain and Mrs. William T. Glidden.[1] Shortly after its consecration on November 22, 1883, the diocesan newspaper published a description of the church by Vaughan:

The style of architecture is Gothic, of the fifteenth century, constructed in what is called "Half-timber work," a mode of building that was prevalent during the fifteenth and sixteenth centuries, and of which there are many fine examples in England still in a very perfect condition. The church is 63 feet in length.[2]

St. Andrew's is thus a rather small church, the nave and chancel forming a rectangle broken only by the small entrance porch on the north side (Vaughan usually avoided transepts and the organizational planning problems they posed).[3] The only external indication of the chancel-nave

23

plan is the shingled belfry with its stubby brooch spire rising from the roof over the first bay of the chancel.[4]

The unassuming exterior is a rare example of rural late English Gothic, even later than Perpendicular, and St. Andrew's is one of the first American buildings to employ half-timbering, a decade or more before its use by such other New England church architects as Frank Bourne, Edwin Lewis, and Cram. The early ecclesiological architects in America had designed churches modeled after rural parish churches in England, but they almost never drew up on "black-and-white" architectural sources from the Welsh borders. Vaughan was therefore a pioneer in the revival of this phase of Gothic—which may have seemed particularly appropriate for Maine, which, like Hereford and Shropshire, might be described as a cultural backwater. None of Vaughan's half-timber buildings were direct copies of English models, although there are certain churches that possibly inspired him, such as Marton Church (St. James, in Vaughan's native Cheshire) and St. Peter's, Melverley, Shropshire (Fig. 13).[5]

The construction cost of $4,000 and Vaughan's statement that St. Andrew's was decorated "in a quiet and simple manner" are somewhat

13. St. Peter's Church, Melverley, Shropshire, c. 1450–1500.

14. St. Andrew's, south wall of chancel, showing stenciling and organ case.

misleading, for the interior of the church gives a singular impression of richness (Figs. 14, 15).[6] This is almost entirely the result of applied decoration, since the rectangular plan is unremarkable in itself. The interior of St. Andrew's, in Vaughan's words,

. . . is divided into seven bays by arches which form the principals of the roof. The chancel consists of two bays and has an arched roof divided by ribs into square panels and decorated with emblems and monograms. The nave has an open timber roof. The walls are plastered to within 4 feet 6 inches from the floor, below that is panelling of wood.[7]

The nave rises to the peak of the roof where the principal rafters are stiffened by arched bracing; there are four simple rafters with purlins. The chancel, on the other hand, does not reach to the ridge of the roof above, but has a lower barrel-vaulted ceiling very much like that of St. Margaret's.

These simple framing members are polychromed (olive with dull red piping—two of Bodley's favorite colors), and they are a part of an overall scheme of elaborate painted stencil work in Vaughan's own hand.[8] The chancel walls are covered with an intricate floriated design (not unlike a Morris wallpaper of this period in its abstraction and two-dimensionality), while the square panels in the chancel ceiling are set off by banded ribs and contain simple floral wreaths which encircle the sacred monograms "IHS" and "A." An enlarged version of the wreath's five-petaled Tudor Rose motif is repeated across the nave ceiling.

Stenciling appeared again in Vaughan's designs, but never as such a dominant decorative feature as in St. Andrew's. Its medieval source is, like the building, fifteenth century, but it was revived by Bodley. Vaughan's master designed the pulpit and screen for Holy Trinity, Cuckfield, Sussex,

15. St. Andrew's Church, interior.

26

16. St. James Church, Old Town, Maine, 1892–1894.

with such a fifteenth-century-style painted roof, and Bodley himself painted patterns on the walls of St. Martin's Scarborough.[9] His office also did other painted ceilings while Vaughan was working there.[10]

The color and richness of the stenciling at St. Andrew's is accentuated by the reredos and organ case. The gilded reredos is a contemporary London recreation of a quattrocento Florentine triptych. The organ case shows the designer's knowledge and exquisite handling of fifteenth-century flamboyant woodwork, for, where funds permitted, Vaughan endowed his churches with carving equaled by few architects of his day.[11] The organ itself is a tracker-action Hutchings. Vaughan, as a product of

27

Tractarianism and the Arts and Crafts Movement, was interested in music; his romantic ecclesiastical designs were ideal settings for the introduction of church music to Puritan New England.[12] Another interior furnishing that Vaughan designed for St. Andrew's, a chancel screen, was never executed.

While interesting historically for its half-timbering, more importantly St. Andrew's demonstrates Vaughan's ability to achieve a pervading religious spirit—St. Andrew's is clearly Victorian, yet it evokes a sense of the past that is found in a church which has served its parish for half a millennium.

St. Andrew's represented a rural church theme which Vaughan was to return to again many times in his career. Even the parish churches constructed without exposed timbers and stucco—such as St. John Evangelist in Tannersville, New York (c. 1884) or St. James Church, Old Town, Maine (1894, Fig. 16)—carried on the practice of austere rectangular plans sheltered beneath long, unbroken roofs.

Both St. James (which is shingled) and St. John have a barrel-vaulted ceiling (as was used only for the chancel at St. Andrew's) running the full length of the nave, and both have simple belfries at their west ends. St. John, built of random fieldstone and clapboards as a summer

17. St. Mary's Church, Penacook, New Hampshire, 1889–1890.

28

chapel for a group of families connected with St. James-the-Less in Philadelphia, is one of Vaughan's simplest ecclesiastical works.[13] The ceiling decorations, similar to those at St. Andrew's, were painted not by Vaughan, but by Father Maynard of the Cowley Fathers.[14]

Another shingled church, St. Mary's (Fig. 17) in Penacook, New Hampshire (1890), a mission church sponsored by St. Paul's School in Concord, is intriguing in that the entrance porch is a large, steeply pitched conical projection which is echoed by a similar but smaller roof that extends out from the peak of the main roof.[15] After the historicism of the Newcastle church, this surprisingly plastic treatment probably stemmed from Vaughan's interest in the then popular Shingle Style and may also reflect his knowledge of American Arts and Crafts designers at this time (for example, Harvey Ellis or the English-born San Francisco architect Ernest Coxhead).

The most important half-timbered churches Vaughan designed after St. Andrew's are Holy Name in Swampscott, Massachusetts; All Saints in Methuen, Massachusetts; and St. Mary's in Northeast Harbor, Maine.[16]

The Church of the Holy Name (Fig. 18) was originally built in 1893 as a summer chapel in the seaside town of Swampscott, just north of Boston.[17] The church is long and narrow, with proportions like those

18. Church of the Holy Name, Swampscott, Massachusetts, 1893.

19. Holy Name, interior.

at Newcastle and Tannersville and the same long expanse of roof beneath an unbroken ridge. Closely spaced vertical timbers accentuate the impression of height and narrowness.

The interior of Holy Name (Fig. 19) has a barrel-vaulted chancel and a six-bay nave, without side aisles, spanned by prominent queen-post, collar-beam wood trusses. The plain walls are offset by wainscoting and a paneled wood reredos is set flush against the east wall. Here the combination of the dark wood and sparkling Kempe glass produces a convincingly medieval atmosphere which, according to R. E. Armstrong, the church's rector, delivers the worshipper "from the disquietude of the world."[18] The massive heaviness of the wood contrasts with the jewel-like quality of the glass and fitments.[19]

Its beauty notwithstanding, Holy Name had a high turnover of priests in its early years, and it was thought that a proper rectory might make the "living" more attractive. In 1907, when Vaughan was asked to build a house next to the church, he unsuccessfully attempted an architecturally harmonious design by grafting a half-timbered tower with a cross motif and quatrefoils onto an otherwise humdrum domestic structure (Fig. 20).[20]

20. Holy Name Rectory,
Swampscott, 1907.

21. All Saints Church, Methuen, Massachusetts, 1904.

31

All Saints (now St. Andrew's) in Methuen (Fig. 21) is a larger
variation of the themes used in the churches at Newcastle and Swampscott. The church is seven bays long and is sheltered by the broad expanse
of slate roof characteristically used by Vaughan. The first bay at the west
is displaced by a tall, square entrance tower, the bottom half of which is
local granite, pierced only by the arched entranceway. The tower's upper
half is composed of narrow and intricate half-timbering with a slim,
triple lancet nestled beneath the squat brooch spire (a slightly more
elongated version of the one at Newcastle). The tower is echoed by a
gabled sacristy in the first bay of the chancel, which reaches to the height
of the main roof.

22. All Saints, interior.

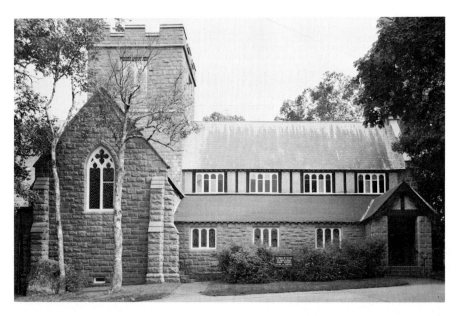

23. St. Mary's-by-the-Sea Church, Northeast Harbor, Maine, 1902.

On the interior (Fig. 22), there is the typical barrel-vaulted chancel, the same timber framing found at Swampscott, and, of course, exquisitely detailed carved furnishings: the paneled reredos with plate tracery, the organ case, and the rood screen. All of the windows have diamond-paned, pale-yellow glass except for Kempe's east window with its muted Pre-Raphaelite greens and reds. All Saints also exhibits the more open plan that Vaughan depended upon when he desired additional seating without sacrificing medieval proportions; the side aisle is separated from the nave by the slimmest of wooden columns.[21]

In his consecration sermon of September 21, 1905, Bishop William Lawrence stressed the importance of the Englishness of All Saints. The sermon was a good illustration of Lawrence's "happy way of laying down an historical background and connecting old England, old Massachusetts and today, and the Episcopal Church as a connecting link between old and new."[22]

Three years before the consecration of the church at Methuen, the Bishop of Maine dedicated one of Vaughan's most intriguing parish churches at the fashionable seaside resort of Northeast Harbor, Mt. Desert Island, Maine. St. Mary's-by-the Sea (Fig. 23) replaced an earlier wooden church of 1882 which had been built at the urging of William Croswell Doane,

Bishop of Albany, and one of the founders of the summer colony of Northeast Harbor.[23] Larger than the earlier structure, the new church crowds its rather constricted site; in fact, the Celtic cross over the present altar marks the grave of Bishop Doane's daughter, which was behind the old church. The small site may account for Vaughan's use of transepts and side aisles, an unusual plan in comparison to the simple rectangles of churches like St. Andrew's or Holy Name.

The rather fragmented design of the granite and half-timbered exterior of St. Mary's is to some degree pulled together by a square tower over the crossing. With the exception of the half-timbered clerestory level of the nave, the church is constructed of local granite laid up in random ashlar, and the simple fenestration (like the single lancet in the transept) hardly interrupts these broad stone surfaces.

24. St. Mary's-by-the-Sea, interior.

The church's pastoral setting is seductive, but it is the interior (Fig. 24) that makes St. Mary's particularly interesting as one of Vaughan's most powerful works. In order to accommodate a large congregation, chairs (which Vaughan almost always favored over pews) were placed across the nave and under the side aisles, which are differentiated here only by lower ceilings and thin columns of the sort associated with Bodley's churches. The nave is spanned by a hammer-beam ceiling, Vaughan's most intricate ceiling, with the exception of St. Mary's, Dorchester (Fig. 25). Offset by pale-yellow walls, the rich warmth of the nave is something of a *tour de force*. Visually separated from the nave by the tall, well-lit crossing, the chancel has a paneled wood ceiling (painted blue with gold stars in the best Bodlean Arts and Crafts tradition) and a large stone cross set flush against the Decorated east window.

25. *St. Mary's Church, Dorchester, Massachusetts, 1888, interior.*

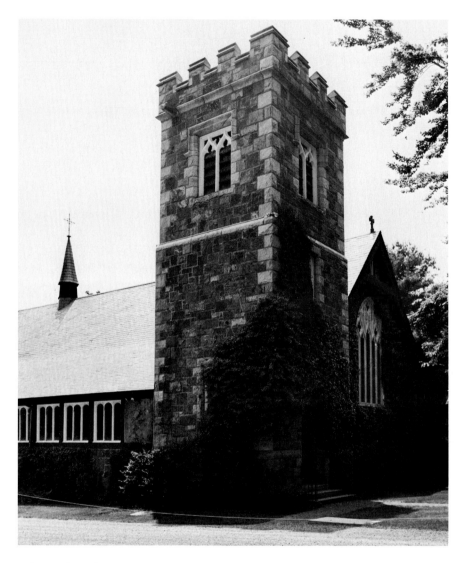

26. St. John's Church, Beverly Farms, Massachusetts, 1902.

St. John's Church in Beverly Farms, Massachusetts (Fig. 26) is similar to St. Mary's in many ways, built in the same year for a fashionable summer colony, and using granite and half-timbering.[24] The church's west end, dominated by a five-part Decorated window and a square, battlemented tower of a warm, yellowish stone, presented the appearance of an English village church such as one finds in the Cotswolds.[25]

36

Vaughan's contribution, the English parish church placed in an American setting, was not just limited to half-timbered buildings. Between 1890 and 1913, Vaughan designed at least seven stone churches, as well as a mission church in brick.[26] Three of these—St. Barnabas in Falmouth and St. Martin's in New Bedford, Massachusetts, and St. Thomas's in Dover, New Hampshire—which were all completed around 1893, form a stylistic trio.

Vaughan's first commission in the 1890s was for St. Barnabas Memorial Church in Falmouth (Fig. 27), which was consecrated on St. Barnabas's Day, 1890, as the "munificent gift" of the family of the late James M. Beebe of Boston.[27] Situated in the center of the village and surrounded by a large open lawn, St. Barnabas is a somewhat different example of Vaughan's work—his first work in stone and apparently the only church to be designed with a stone spire.[28] In some respects, St. Barnabas anticipates later commissions, while at the same time its exterior is among Vaughan's least felicitous designs.

27. St. Barnabas Church and Parish House, Falmouth, Massachusetts, 1889–1890.

37

28. St. Barnabas, interior.

St. Barnabas has a squat and chunky appearance, an impression which is heightened by the large ashlar blocks of gray granite with dark red sandstone trim—the whole effect being reminiscent of the work of Richardson. A simple spire (perhaps specified by the donor) is perched on top of a Decorated west tower with angled corner buttressing.

Vaughan's church plans are rarely cruciform and the exterior elevations are almost never symmetrical, but at St. Barnabas the whole scheme seems unnecessarily disjointed, lacking the unity of his half-timbered churches and collegiate chapels. The different heights of the entrance porch, sacristy, and vestry in a church clearly visible from all sides are a bit arbitrary. However, St. Barnabas does demonstrate Vaughan's ability to handle large areas of blank wall, while the long, unbroken ridge of the roof partially counteracts the overall disunity.

The awkwardness of the exterior is compensated for by the simplicity and strength of the interior (Fig. 28). After the richness of Swampscott and Newcastle, St. Barnabas could be called austere, with decoration

38

limited to the chancel. In the nave, there is wainscoting to the base of the windows, but above that the stucco walls are absolutely plain. The simple pews and bare walls only serve to emphasize the real glory of the church—its wooden ceiling—which has a wagon roof of eight massive trusses with straight rafters continuing up to the ridge of the roof.

The middle church of this stone triad is St. Thomas's in Dover (Fig. 29).[29] As at the Falmouth church of the year before, Vaughan again played

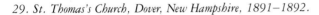

29. St. Thomas's Church, Dover, New Hampshire, 1891–1892.

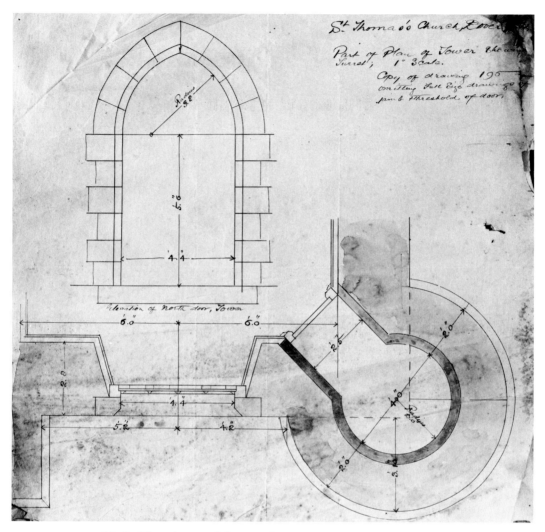

30. *St. Thomas's, part of the tower plan.*

with large areas of blank wall. There is also the all-important large expanse of roof at St. Thomas's; but here the spireless tower is integrated more fully with the body of the church. The tower has a round, turretlike stair and is topped by a conical spire with an applied decorative cross (Fig. 30).

The west elevation of the church resembles a right triangle standing on its short side, the hypotenuse defined by the conical turret, the inside corner of the tower, the peak of the nave roof, and the bottom of the aisle roof. The total effect of St. Thomas's shows its indebtedness to the Arts and Crafts Movement. Vaughan's asymmetrical west wall composition,

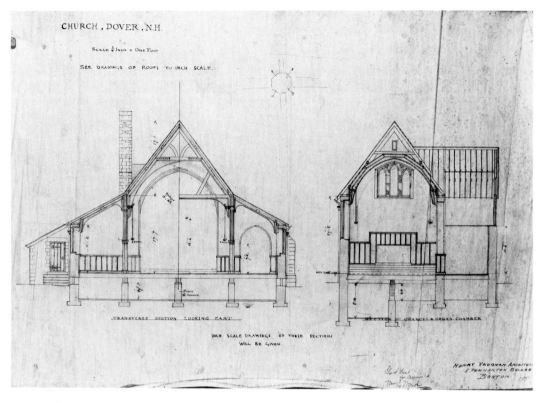

31. St. Thomas's, transverse section looking east; section of chancel and organ chamber.

for example, recalls the contemporaneous work in England of C. F. A. Voysey, an architect who, like Vaughan, looked to vernacular buildings of the Middle Ages for inspiration.[30]

St. Thomas's Church was built as the result of a competition to replace an 1840 wooden Gothic meeting house demolished by eminent domain for a new town hall.[31] William A. Niles, Bishop of New Hampshire, laid the cornerstone for the new church on July 29, 1891. A special meeting of the vestry a year earlier had contracted for the building of a church and chapel "according to the plans of Mr. Henry Vaughan of Boston."[32] Due to the similarity of program and style, it is hardly surprising that this church is like St. Barnabas, except that the larger congregation of St. Thomas's necessitated side aisles resulting in a more open plan than at the Falmouth church. The interior has a wooden barrel-vaulted chancel with tall reredos against the east wall, and the six-bay nave is spanned by king post, tie-beam trusses which extend to the ridge (Fig. 31). The trusses are supported by thin octagonal wood columns, which allows the seating of a large congregation without reverting to

41

transepts while still retaining a proper ecclesiological feeling.[33] As at St. Barnabas, the wood trussing (offset by unadorned stucco walls) is the church's main strength; with the exception of the reredos, there is almost no decoration.

The third of the stone churches from the early 1890s is St. Martin's, in the old whaling seaport of New Bedford. The cornerstone was laid in June 1891, but construction was slow and only the nave was completed at the time of the first service in the spring of 1892. An essay in decorated or fourteenth-century Gothic, St. Martin's was never completed, although

32. St. Martin's Church, New Bedford, Massachusetts, 1891–1892.

an 1893 drawing shows how Vaughan intended the church to look (Fig. 32).[34]

The proposed church is almost a mirror image of St. Thomas's, although the tower was halted halfway up and gabled. Again, there is an asymmetrical end wall (not unlike a New England saltbox), which, with its single Decorated window, is the church's most satisfactory aspect. The simple window openings displace only a minimum of wall space, while every surface of the light-gray granite shows Vaughan's delight in working with large areas of blank wall.

33. Christ Church, Swansea, Massachusetts, 1899–1900.

Unfinished and lacking the bucolic small-town setting of St. Thomas's, St. Martin's almost seems to be the neo-Perpendicular church by G. G. Scott, Jr., Bodley, or Austin & Paley described by the English critic and poet John Betjeman:

You will remember it in some suburb of a provincial town where you stayed with an aunt, or on holiday in the outskirts of a southcoast watering place, and you can read of it in Compton Mackenzie's *Sinister Street*. "Tingting" the single bell calls to Sung Eucharist, because the tower, designed for a full peal of bells, was never completed. Rather gaunt without it, the church rises above the privet and forsythia . . . for there is no churchyard to these churches; we have reached the era of municipal cemeteries. . . . The chief beauty of the church is in its proportions.[35]

Close to St. Martin's, both geographically and stylistically, is Christ Church, Swansea, Massachusetts, consecrated by Bishop Lawrence in June 1900 (Fig. 33). Built with a bequest of $20,000, the church was the gift of Frank S. Stevens, an acquaintance of Vaughan's who made his fortune in the stagecoach business in California following the gold rush in 1849.[36] The crenelated west tower with conical stair tower, as well as the lone Decorated-style window, recall St. Martin's. The dominant mass of slate roof is present, and the fenestration is typically small in relation to the light-colored granite wall surface. The interior (Fig. 34) features the basic ingredients of a plain nave spanned by arch-beamed trusses, a deep chancel with a cradle ceiling, exquisitely carved furniture (including a Hutchings organ), and a typical, shimmering Kempe window over the tall, paneled reredos.

Bishop Lawrence singled out Christ Church, Swansea, in his obituary of Vaughan.[37] In his consecration sermon, Lawrence had spoken at some length about the church's architecture as an expression of Episcopalianism in America. Aware of its roots in New England Puritanism, he defended the appropriateness of the Gothic style to modern New England:

The architecture and its contrast with the classic style of old New England suggests a change that has come over the people. Many of them are turning back to the prayer book, the dignified forms and rich associations of the church of our English ancestors . . . A modern aesthetic taste, an historic sense, and a love of ancient traditions, drove them back to the ecclesiastical architecture of old England.[38]

The indefatigable Bishop of Massachusetts (who seems to have done prac-

34. *Christ Church, chancel.*

tically nothing but consecrate Vaughan churches) also declared that the architect's new church for St. John's parish in Newtonville (1902–1903, Fig. 35) was

. . . an excellent simple type of suburban church. Gothic in architecture and beautifully furnished within and without, the building does much by the simple dignity of its lines to give inspiration to all who worship within its walls.[39]

45

35. St. John's Church, Newtonville, Massachusetts, 1902.

36. Church of the Redeemer, Chestnut Hill, Massachusetts, 1913–1915; tower completed 1920

It is rather in another Boston suburb that Vaughan built his last, largest, and perhaps finest parish church—a fitting ending to a story that began with St. Andrew's, Newcastle. The Church of the Redeemer in

46

37. *Church of the Redeemer, consecration of the first church, June 1, 1891.*

38. *Church of the Redeemer,*
drawing of the west end.

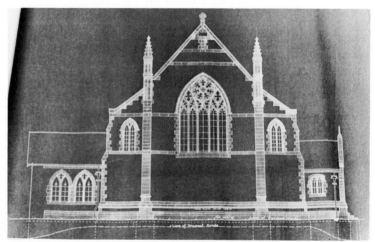

Chestnut Hill (1913–1915, Fig. 36) is a skillful combination of a large city church and a small country parish, retaining the attributes of both (the church has a seating capacity of 350 within a nave that measures 123 by 50 feet).[40] The warm local brownstone, the late Decorated body of the church, and the Perpendicular tower make the Redeemer an almost text-book example of the change from the colorful complexity of the Victorian Gothic to the disciplined and restrained correctness of the Modern Gothic style. This is especially evident when the present structure is compared to its 1891 predecessor, with its open, meeting-house plan covered in shingles and capped by a spire (Fig. 37).

47

Vaughan's large double-aisled Church of the Redeemer has a variety of features, like pinnacled buttresses, a circular stair tower, and the elaborate reticulated west window, all of which are skillfully integrated to give an impression of harmony. The architect's control is evident in the west window, where the complex tracery is framed by the large area of blank wall (Fig. 38).

The most successful portion of the Redeemer is the tower. The tower originally proposed for the church, shown in an illustration in the *Church Militant* of March 1913 (Fig. 39), is almost identical to the one Vaughan designed for the Church of the Mediator in New York two years before. This design also recalls Bodley's St. John's, Epping, of 1889, a fact that emphasizes the continuing close relationship Vaughan maintained with his mentor.

When the estimated cost of the Redeemer, exclusive of tower, organ, glass, and furnishings, was found to be $80,000, it was decided to postpone the construction of the tower.[41] Though an additional $20,000 was offered by two parishioners, "after consultation with the architect," it was decided that a tower could not be built for such a sum.[42] In May of 1916, exactly one year after the church's consecration, the Building

39. Church of the Redeemer, watercolor elevation showing first tower design.

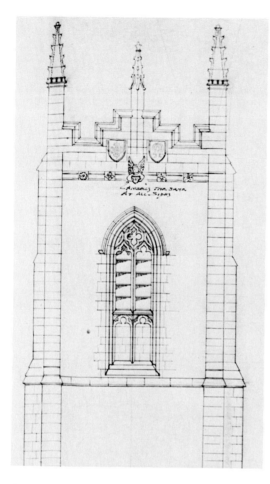

40. Church of the Redeemer, drawing of the tower, second design.

Committee was instructed to obtain an estimate for the tower from Vaughan, though it was not until June of 1918 that all drawings pertaining to the church were "procured from the estate of Henry Vaughan Architect."[43]

These papers include blueprints of the original design for the tower, as well as ink drawings of the tower as it was actually built (Fig. 40). Dedicated by Bishop Lawrence on October 31, 1920, the "Victory Tower" retains the basic three-stage Perpendicular configuration of the original design, but with significant modifications. The simple battlements are replaced with stepped ones, the buttresses are extended up to the pinnacles, and the double belfry openings are replaced with a single one (Fig. 41). Beneath the parapet, forming the corbel of a secondary pinnacle, is the shield-carrying angel found at St. Swithun's at Magdalen College, Oxford, of 1880 that Vaughan used almost as his signature. The result is a more refined, less chunky, and far richer Perpendicular tower than the earlier design. The use of the Perpendicular tower grafted onto the slightly

49

41. *Church of the Redeemer.*

42. Church of the Redeemer, interior.

earlier Decorated nave is a stroke of genius, for Vaughan's composition captures the transitory moment when a declining style foretells the ascendancy of a newer style.[44]

The interior of the Redeemer (Fig. 42) is one of Vaughan's most majestic spatial compositions. Vaughan's use of side aisles (which are merely passageways and are as tall as the nave), internal buttresses, and continuous nave-chancel ceiling, makes reference to some of his later city and collegiate churches (for example, Good Shepherd in New York and Western Reserve Chapel in Cleveland), and the "hall church" effect is not

51

43. *Bodley & Garner, St. Augustine's, Pendlebury, interior.*

unlike Bodley's Epping Church or his masterpiece, St. Augustine's, Pendlebury (Fig. 43). The four-bay nave and the two-bay chancel lie beneath an unbroken roof line, but Vaughan avoided a tunnel-like impression by setting off the side aisles with tall stone arches which reach nearly to the roof plate (there is no clerestory). A small morning chapel is nestled to the side of the chancel at the east end of the south aisle. Characteristically, the power of the Redeemer's interior relies on stately proportions and the contrast of the plain walls of the nave with the rich, decorative treatment of the chancel.

The Church of the Redeemer, like almost all of the architect's parish churches (for example, St. Mary's, Dorchester, Fig. 44), shows that Vaughan succeeded in providing a suitable framework for Christian worship—monuments dedicated to the glory of God—both suited to contemporary needs and strongly rooted in tradition. Once again, the words of Bishop Lawrence eloquently speak of Vaughan's aims and convictions:

While religious faith is revealed in life and creed, it also is expressed through our churches. Hence the construction of a church of beauty and dignity in this diocese is welcomed as a symbol of the living faith of the people and their appreciation of the dignity and beauty of worship.[45]

44. St. Mary's, Dorchester.

3

CITY CHURCHES
AND CATHEDRALS

*In the city church {ecclesiastical architecture} obtains its fullest chance of showing its adaptability
to conditions essentially modern and almost without precedent. It is here that Christian architecture
is privileged to prove its extreme adaptability, its vitality, its power of fitting itself to new conditions
without losing any of its historic and spiritual qualities.*

Ralph Adams Cram

IT WOULD be nice to claim that Henry Vaughan, the master of the
country church, redirected the city church, but the truth is simply that
he attempted to produce the same effect in his urban work as he sought
in all his other ecclesiastical architecture. And in this he generally succeeded.
Two city churches—Christ Church in New Haven, Connecticut, and the
Church of the Good Shepherd in New York City—are among Vaughan's
most accomplished ecclesiastical designs.

Vaughan's work at St. Margaret's in Boston led to his selection as
the architect for another city church, the Mission Church of the Holy
Cross in New York City. Holy Cross was built for an independent English-
women's society modeled on the Cowley Fathers, the St. John Baptist
Foundation. This group conducted missionary activities among the German-
speaking tenement dwellers of Manhattan's East Side. They were assisted
in this by three priests, James Otis Huntington, son of the Bishop of
Central New York, and two assistants, all of whom had been with the
Cowley Fathers at Oxford. (Huntington had also served at the Church of
the Advent in Boston, the bridgehead for Anglo-Catholicism in New
England, and probably knew Vaughan there.) Father Huntington's
missionary work led to the founding of the Order of the Holy Cross, the
first purely American religious order for men.[1] After unsuccessfully offer-
ing to join with the local parish, the Church of the Nativity, the Foundation decided to erect its own building.[2] Vaughan was named the archi-

54

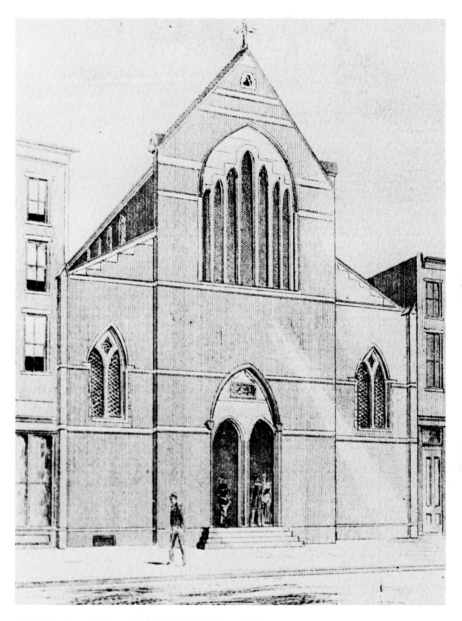

45. *Holy Cross Mission Church, New York City, 1885.*

tect, and the cornerstone was laid on May 3, 1885.[3] Rapidly completed, the church was consecrated on September 14, 1885, the Festival of the Exaltation of the Cross.[4]

Located at 4th Street and Avenue C, Holy Cross was used by the Foundation until about World War I, when, because of the changing

46. *Holy Cross Mission Church, interior.*

nature of the order, the society moved to Mendham, New Jersey. At that time the building was sold to a Roman Catholic congregation and, still later, pulled down, leaving only a few views as evidence of its appearance, such as those in the *New York Daily Graphic* of September 17, 1885, which appeared at the time of its dedication by Bishop Henry Codman Potter (Figs. 45, 46).[5]

Holy Cross apparently had an extremely simple brick facade reflecting the basilican plan behind it. The walls were plain except for a large, seven-lancet west window, double lancets at the ends of the side aisles, and a pointed-arch entrance. Its rather stark two-dimensional exterior

47. St. Bartholomew's Church, Cambridge, Massachusetts, 1892.

seems more like an early nineteenth-century Gothic Revival church than one of the picturesque and colorful Victorian examples of the 1870s—to say nothing of Vaughan's other work. This probably reflected the Ecclesiological philosophy of appropriateness—a simple mission should not appear overbearing or out of keeping with its neighborhood.

The interior of Holy Cross was more typically Vaughan, with the omnipresent barrel-vaulted ceiling, a windowless east wall, and a late English Gothic carved reredos and pulpit. The chancel is slightly elevated and a large rood is perched upon a simple cross beam. Holy Cross is unusual in Vaughan's work in that it has a clerestory above the nave

57

arcade (necessitated by the windowless side aisles). The long nave (five bays are visible in old photographs) with its simple pointed arches and octagonal columns is very Bodlean.[6] The church is remarkable for the quiet dignity derived from structural materials and spatial arrangements rather than for elaborate furnishings or colorful glass. Compared with much American church architecture of the time—such as John Sturgis's Church of the Advent in Boston, or even Richardson's Trinity Church—the interior of Holy Cross must have seemed exceedingly chaste.[7]

The Cambridge Tribune of March 5, 1892, carried a story of the ground breaking for another mission church, St. Bartholomew's, in that Massachusetts city. The account, accompanied by the architect's elevation of the west facade (Fig. 47), described the church and gave its dimensions:

The nave will be 70 by 34. The chancel 22 by 19. . . . The nave will accommodate 360 adults . . . the exterior will be shingled. . . . The interior walls are to be plastered. . . . The roof timbers are to be exposed . . . the height of the spire from street grade to top of cross, 83 feet 5 inches.[8]

The design of St. Bartholomew's (which was to minister to underprivileged workers and West Indians) is very similar to that of St. James, Old Town, Maine, of 1894 (Fig. 16), both shingled churches featuring a square tower and octagonal open belfry.[9]

With construction of Christ Church, New Haven (Figs. 48, 49) Vaughan demonstrated that he was a worthy successor to Street, Pearson, and Bodley. Christ Church boasts one of America's great Gothic Revival interiors, while the tower was the prototype for countless churches and college chapels. Vaughan designed everything structural and decorative, and the result is a fairly complete statement of his faith in the Gothic.

Christ Church was originally a Gothic-style chapel of Trinity Church (itself a monument in an earlier revival of English medieval forms), but by 1879 the 600-seat wooden structure of 1860 was insufficient, so the expanding parish organized a fund-raising drive for a new church. By July 1894, $33,000 had been raised, and by October the new church was considered a certainty. The foundation stone was laid on St. Mark's Day, 1895, and the new church was consecrated May 26, 1898.[10]

Situated on a triangular lot adjacent to Yale University, Christ Church is basically a long, narrow, rectangular block constructed of Connecticut Valley (Longmeadow) brownstone and dominated by a tall, almost free-standing tower. The asymmetrical east end (Fig. 50) exhibits sacristy and morning-chapel roofs of markedly different heights. The chancel wall,

48. Christ Church,
New Haven, Connecticut,
1895–1898, east end.

49. Christ Church, plan.

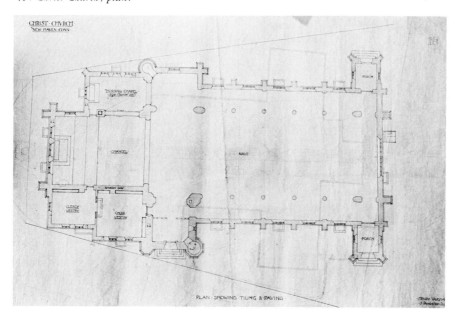

50. *Christ Church, east elevation.*

framed by buttresses, features a triple-lancet arrangement filled with Decorated tracery.

Before construction began, Eldon Deane, a well-known late-nineteenth-century architectural renderer, made a watercolor elevation of Christ Church (Fig. 51) which shows light-colored stone deployed for the facing of the buttresses, for the window quoins, and for the tower pinnacles.

51. Christ Church, watercolor by Eldon Deane.

Contrasting with the darker brownstone, this trim has a decidedly Victorian effect; it is almost a glance backward to the 1870s. Vaughan in fact used monochromatic masonry, making a handsomer, more assured composition.

Vaughan also radically changed the design of the tower (Fig. 52) from that shown in the Deane rendering. The earlier tower had one of the pinnacles topped with a miniature spire and decorative cross, rather

52. *Christ Church, tower.*

like an enlarged version of the tower at St. Thomas's, Dover. Vaughan
abandoned this picturesque Arts and Crafts motif for a close adaptation
of the tower at Magdalen College, Oxford (1492–1507, Fig. 53).[11]

Vaughan could hardly have chosen a better model. As in the tower
at Oxford, Vaughan limited decoration to the upper half of the tower.
More important, the monumental tower dramatically proclaims the church:

53. Magdalen Tower, Magdalen College, Oxford, c. 1500.

it is the most successful element in Christ Church's design and constitutes a focal point in the New Haven skyline. As for his school chapels, Vaughan undoubtedly considered that an English collegiate model was most appropriate for an American academic setting. The tower at Christ Church was the first in a long line of "Magdalens" employed for city churches and on American college campuses.[12] The references to Oxford seem particularly apt in New Haven today where the view toward Yale reveals several later Gothic towers.

In writing of the ideal city church, Cram singled out Vaughan's New Haven work as a

. . . church worked out on lines that are absolutely right. There is the loftiness of the walls and the perfect simplicity of parts that must always mark a city church that is conceived with due regard to its environment. Moreover, it has that singular refinement, that courtly self-respect, that seems indispensable. It could not be taken for a country church; yet is pure and scholarly Gothic, both modern in feeling and medieval—the enduring style adapted to new conditions.[13]

The interior of Christ Church (Fig. 54) is as handsome as the exterior. The nave is six bays long and the chancel three. Behind a tall, sharply pointed nave arcade stand low side aisles with wooden lean-to roofs; the arch closest to the chancel is taller and reaches into the clerestory level. The other arches are surmounted by double lancets recessed into simple openings. The chancel (offset by an elaborate rood and screen) culminates in a Winchester-type screen reredos containing three levels of figures beneath individual canopies flanking the crucifix. The nave seating consists of chairs, an early instance of their use in this country.[14] The ceiling is a cradle roof with closely spaced tie-beams between the bays.

Like most Vaughan churches, the immediate impression conveyed by Christ Church is one of sumptuousness. Vaughan's use of red brick for the walls gives a feeling of conspicuous warmth which is accentuated by the brownstone trim and the wood ceiling and furnishings, as well as by the soft greenish glow of the Kempe glass.[15] The warm hues of these simple materials contrast with the lighter Caen stones employed for the reredos and sedilia, the Knoxville marble of the altar, and the Carrara marble chancel floor. Marble stations of the cross line the walls of the nave.[16]

While Christ Church is basically freestanding, the Church of the Good Shepherd (1902–1903) on East 31st Street in New York City, forced Vaughan to tackle a siting problem like the one he encountered at Holy Cross. Commissioned by the Church of the Incarnation on Madison

54. Christ Church, interior.

*55. Christ Church,
detail of tower angel.*

65

56. *Church of the Good Shepherd, New York City, 1902–1903, and Brooks Parish House, 1901–1902.*

Avenue, the red brick chapel and parish house were designed as a single unit (Fig. 56). Intended as a memorial to a recently deceased rector of the Incarnation, the Arthur Brooks Parish House was begun slightly earlier (1901–1902) than the church when an initial contribution of $20,000 was augmented by numerous other gifts. The cornerstone of the church was laid on April 19, 1902. [17]

Arthur Brooks was the brother of Phillips Brooks, Rector of Trinity Church and William Lawrence's immediate predecessor as Bishop of Massachusetts. Thus, the Parish of the Incarnation had strong links with the Boston Anglo-Catholic community. But this only partly explains the choice of Vaughan as architect to design the new church. Perhaps more important, Incarnation had a tradition of employing major artists (the

66

parent church has memorials by Richardson and the American sculptor Augustus Saint-Gaudens, among others). The parish's commissioning of a non-New York architect, relatively unknown outside of High Church circles, shows the stylistic change in ecclesiastical architecture and points up Vaughan's position as a preferred designer for socially prominent and artistically conscious Episcopal churches.

"Brooks House" constitutes two-thirds of a three-part composition, with the west facade of the church and the tall gable-end of the parish house framing the slightly recessed central portion. The whole block is a bit like an H-plan Elizabethan prodigy house compressed into a single plane. Despite Gothic detailing, the fenestration of the central portion is rather classical and consists of five arches topped by two rows of five paired windows each. The windows and the corners of the parish house have light-colored stone quoins, and three shields and a date stone are featured on the facade. Brooks House contained a gymnasium, library, and other community service facilities.[18]

The church and parish house are visually unified by stone bands that run the width of both facades, creating a strong horizontal emphasis. However, the narrow saddleback tower rising on the church's south side emphasizes the dominance of the church. Given the limitations of a single facade, Vaughan created a composition that is anything but two-dimensional; Vaughan's 31st Street church is a subtle and successful solution to the problem of ecclesiastical design in the middle of a city block.

Although individual features derive from nineteenth-century English sources, the facade of Good Shepherd is among Vaughan's most original and satisfying church exteriors. The tower is a type used by Butterfield, Street, and occasionally by Bodley (for example, All Saints, Selsley, Gloucestershire). The banding was used by all three architects, while the proportions of the west wall composition is reminiscent of Groton, as well as Bodley's Queens' College Chapel, Cambridge.

Vaughan knew the urban churches of his English contemporaries first hand and recalled them here, particularly Butterfield in his almost capricious juxtaposition of the ornate tower with the plain body of the church (Vaughan rarely allowed decoration of any kind to interfere with the large expanse of wall he loved). Detailing, such as the crockets and finials over the entranceway (where a pair of "St. Swithun's angels" are found like those at the Redeemer and at New Haven, Figs. 40, 55, 57) and the magnificent Decorated window, exhibits a slight dryness that appeared in some of his work after 1900. However, the exterior as a whole, with its use of contrasting brick and stone, picturesque tower, and

67

almost playful angels, shows Vaughan's continued debt to the Arts and Crafts tradition.

The interior of the Church of the Good Shepherd (Fig. 58) recalls certain earlier works, notably St. Paul's School Chapel and Christ Church, New Haven, and perhaps Holy Cross. Like a late-English collegiate chapel in plan, the chancel has the same tall height and dimensions as the nave and is defined only by a stone arch; there is no rood screen to obscure the view of the altar and Kempe window. As at New Haven, there are tall

57. *Good Shepherd, entrance detail.*

58. *Good Shepherd, interior.*

59. Church of the Mediator, Bronx, New York, 1911.

nave arcades, but here they define two small chapels rather than side aisles or additional seating. The walls are plain stucco, and the rich decoration—window tracery, reredos, and organ case—is kept to a minimum. The ceiling is spanned by a simple cradle roof (which may explain Good Shepherd's excellent acoustics).[19] While the interior of Good Shepherd lacks some of the warmth and picturesque quality of Christ Church, New Haven, its sense of suave self-assurance and architectural correctness marks Vaughan as Bodley's American heir.[20]

Vaughan's other New York City work is the Church of the Mediator (Fig. 59) in the Kingsbridge section of the Bronx. In its appearance as a freestanding building with a tower, it is similar to the Church of the Redeemer. Yet, in its size and dominance of the neighborhood, it can be considered a city church. Built in 1911, the Mediator is constructed of gray fieldstone—a material favored by Vaughan's Modern Gothic successors, but unusual in Vaughan's work and not as warm as the stone of his other churches. The body of the church is a tall, rectangular block that

70

harks back to the chapel of St. Paul's and Bodlean churches such as St. Michael's, Camden Town, London (Fig. 60). The west end is unique because the entrance porch projects out from the center of the wall beneath the large windows—where Vaughan usually preferred to employ a blank expanse of wall—which is perhaps a concession to the constricted urban lot.

60. Bodley & Garner, St. Michael's Church, Camden Town, London, 1876–1881.

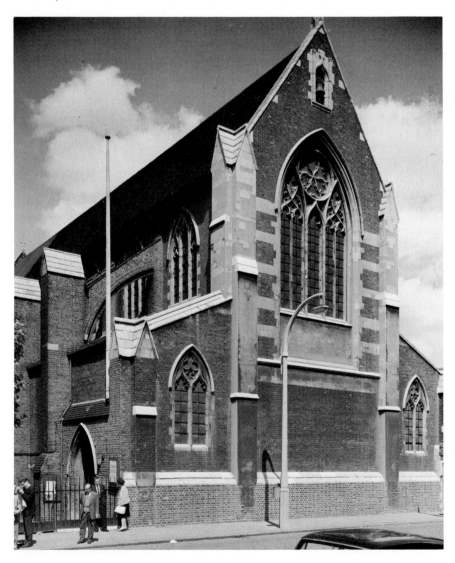

61. Mediator, interior (taken in 1914, before the installation of the stained glass).

The Mediator is also Vaughan's only church with a tower at its east end. Compared to New Haven or the Redeemer, the three-stage Perpendicular tower (with its double lancets and simple crenelated cornice) seems rather chunky. The exterior of the Mediator is properly English, but it seems slightly mechanical and lacks the passion of Vaughan's greater works.[21]

Inside, the Mediator unexpectedly sheds the dry quality of the outside (Fig. 61). The large nave is similar to the one at Good Shepherd, except that there is no clerestory and the full-height nave arcade screens side aisles which are actually only narrow passageways cut into the piers or internal buttresses. The deep and narrow chancel is not as tall or as wide as the nave, from which it is offset by a simple stone arch. The most notable aspect of the church is the monumental screen-form reredos hovering above the altar, incorporating painted panels as well as carved figures in niches and covering most of the east wall beneath a rose window. The exterior of the Church of the Mediator looks as if it were built in the second decade of this century, but the interior reminds us that Vaughan was still very much Bodley's disciple.

The last ten years of Vaughan's life were largely devoted to work on the National Cathedral, as well as to extensive work at the Cathedral of St. John the Divine in New York City. The Washington commission was done with Bodley, so that Vaughan's training, architectural philosophy, and role as emissary of Bodley's style in America came to a logical conclusion in the joint work of the two old friends and fellow Anglo-Catholics. While the nearly completed Washington Cathedral is more properly the work of later architects, the cathedral commission marked an important chapter in Vaughan's career.

Washington Cathedral—or the Cathedral of Saint Peter and Saint Paul—was to nominally serve the new diocese of Washington, which had been created and separated from Maryland in 1895. But in actuality it was the fruition of a long-felt desire to have a *national cathedral* in the nation's capital. Even before the new diocese was formed, Congress chartered the Protestant Episcopal Cathedral Foundation of the District of Columbia (1893), granting it the power to establish a cathedral.[22] The physical realization of this dream for a national house of worship took shape under Washington's first bishop, Henry Yates Satterlee, whose bishopric (1896–1908) was wholeheartedly devoted to the founding and building of the cathedral.

In addition to the task of generating funds, Bishop Satterlee was most concerned with the choice of an architect and a style for the cathedral. In the 1890s Ernest Flagg was commissioned to produce both Renaissance and Gothic designs for a cathedral, and as late as 1906 an Advisory Committee recommended a "Classic Renaissance" design. But the opinion of committee members Charles McKim and Daniel Burnham, who both favored a Renaissance building, was overruled by the Board of Trustees, who voted to secure Gothic plans, not by competition, but from an American architect, "preferably neither Beaux-Arts trained, brilliant, young, nor conceited." The Trustees' Committee on the Cathedral Building then asked four architects known for their Gothic work to submit designs of Gothic churches actually completed. Those invited were Charles Haight, Robert Gibson, Ralph Adams Cram, and Henry Vaughan, whose chapels at Groton and St. Paul's were called "two of the most beautiful Gothic churches in America."[23]

It should not, however, be assumed that Satterlee's desire for a cathedral in the Gothic style was purely the result of personal preference. Rather, Washington Cathedral can be seen as another manifestation of a worldwide wave of English Gothic cathedral building. William Burges erected an Anglican cathedral in the Irish city of Cork in the 1860s, while Scott built St. Mary's Cathedral, Edinburgh, and designed other cathedrals, including one for Bombay. The construction of so many English Gothic cathedrals overseas can be understood as a logical extension of the British Empire, as the forms inspired by Lincoln, Wells, and Gloucester appeared in such places as Australia, the Far East, and even the Falkland Islands. Bodley himself produced cathedrals for Hobart, Tasmania, and for San Francisco, following the 1906 earthquake. There was precedent for Bishop Satterlee's insistence upon English Gothic for an American cathedral in the selection of Englishman Robert Gibson over such native talent as Richardson for the cathedral in Albany. In short, the late nineteenth century was a golden age of cathedral construction, the last major English Gothic commission being Liverpool, a competition won by Scott's grandson in 1903. This "cathedral age" was in many ways the climax— some would say the last gasp—of the Gothic Revival.

Although he recognized that an American architect was requisite for an American cathedral, Bishop Satterlee believed that the "paramount consideration" was the "*personality* of the architect," by which he meant not originality, but religious enthusiasm coupled with architectural knowledge.[24] Satterlee's trip to England in search of such an architect was greeted with several strong endorsements of Bodley. The Bishop of Liverpool, who was in the process of erecting an even larger cathedral (of which Bodley was consulting architect), recommended Vaughan's mentor, while the Archbishop of Canterbury assured him that Bodley was "the foremost Gothic architect in England." Even the American Gothicist architect William Appleton Potter, whom Satterlee met in Rome, agreed that Bodley "was recognized by all to be the leading living English architect."[25] Thus the ideal solution seemed to be the joint appointment of Bodley and Vaughan, or as the Committee phrased it:

In as much as Mr. Bodley stands acknowledged by all at the head of English Gothic architects, and as Mr. Vaughan (formerly a pupil in the office of Mr. Bodley), has the highest kind of endorsement from prominent American clergymen, for whom he has built Gothic Churches, your Committee recommend that Mr. Henry Vaughan of Boston and Mr. George F. Bodley of London be employed as architects.[26]

On October 8, 1906, the Cathedral Chapter, through Satterlee, wrote Vaughan to announce their selection of him and Bodley as "the associate architects who are to build the cathedral."[27]

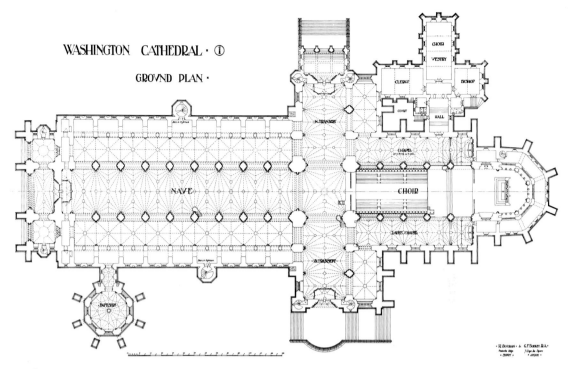

62. *Bodley & Vaughan, Washington Cathedral, plan, 1907.*

On September 29, 1907, with Vaughan present, the foundation stone of the Cathedral of Saint Peter and Saint Paul was laid. The year prior to this ceremony was spent in preparing the preliminary designs, with Vaughan's sailing to England to assist Bodley early in 1907.[28] The general design for the cathedral which had been adopted by the chapter cannot have been in any way adequate for the construction of such a large and complicated structure. In fact, Vaughan and Bodley understood that funds for the design might not be forthcoming and that the chapter wanted a design they could "show to people."[29] At the time of Bodley's death on October 21, 1907, the National Cathedral existed as "a single set of line drawings in ink on heavy white paper" in Vaughan's Boston office.[30]

These first plans, accepted on June 10, 1907, were received not without criticism. But, despite their incompleteness and obvious deficiencies, they show Bodley and Vaughan's original conception.[31] The basic fourteenth-century plan is cruciform with a central tower supported by four great piers at the crossing and two towers at the west end.[32] This plan (Fig. 62) is typically English (like Wells, for example), being rather spread out with a long nave (nine bays), narrow crossing with short

75

transepts, a choir flanked by narrow side chapels, and a polygonal apse. Other noticeable features are the heavy, complex piers, the lack of western aisles in the transept arms, and a shallow narthex. Also, the buttresses do not extend beyond the lower aisle wall, leaving the exterior nave outline unbroken and creating the impression of an unusually compact design.

This taut, skintight, two-dimensional quality (perhaps heightened in drawings) is even more evident in the design of the exterior (Fig. 63). The brittleness that characterizes some of Vaughan's work after the turn of the century is apparent, but the flatness and the impression that major components are all formed with right angles is probably the result of the architects' love of exploiting broad masses and placing small window openings in large wall areas. Neither Bodley nor Vaughan ever conceived a church as merely a frame for glass (as in French Gothic), and despite the skillful window-wall relationships, one suspects that there would not be enough glass to properly illuminate a cathedral of such dimensions.

The pervading sense of wall in the work of these two architects

63. Bodley & Vaughan, Washington Cathedral, southeast elevation, 1907.

64. *Washington Cathedral, model, c. 1916–1917.*

steeped in English medieval architecture is extended to the central tower, the building's most prominent feature. The four pinnacles that frame the tower are smooth and unbroken by detailing. The three lancets, in shallow recesses between the square pinnacles, appear to be punched from the thin, unbattlemented wall that holds them.[33]

In addition to the sense of wall, the original designs reveal the architects' continuing reliance upon their Arts and Crafts background. The drawings abound with little "nonclassical" Gothic elements, asymmetrical details, and inconsistencies. For example, the turretlike stair towers (leading to the triforium) on each side of the exterior nave wall are not directly opposite each other, but are set one bay apart, while the transept, having only an east aisle, also produces an asymmetrical exterior configuration. Such deliberate asymmetry was carried further, as illustrated by a comparison of the north and south elevations (Figs. 64, 65). The primary buttress pinnacles framing the south transept are flat and square (echoing those of the tower) and terminate with crocketed finials. Yet the corresponding piers for the north transept are polygonal turrets topped with chevron-incised roofs that are shorter than the finials on the south transept.

65. Bodley & Vaughan, Washington Cathedral, south elevation, 1907.

No one, least of all Vaughan, expected such preliminary plans to remain unaltered, but it was the drawings for the west end that caused the greatest consternation (Fig. 66). From the outset, Bishop Satterlee was unhappy with the original design of the west front, for he felt it was not monumental enough for the cathedral's main approach.[34] Even more than the tower, the west front exhibited the flat, two-dimensional quality of the Groton chapel and Good Shepherd. The emphasis given by the towers was decidedly vertical, and, except for the decoration applied to their upper stages, the effect was one of "wall." The three portals, although tall and deeply recessed, appeared to have been hewn from the masonry mass. These portals also had the disadvantage of not letting much light into the nave.

There is at least one drawing for the cathedral interior done by Vaughan and Bodley (Fig. 67). Also, a set of drawings of the proposed cathedral developed from the Englishmen's plans was prepared by Donald

66. *Bodley & Vaughan, Washington Cathedral, west elevation, 1907.*

67. *Bodley & Vaughan, Washington Cathedral, drawing of nave looking east, 1907.*

68. *Washington Cathedral, drawing of nave from south transept, c. 1923, by Donald Robb (based on Bodley & Vaughan's preliminary design as developed by Frohman, Robb & Little).*

69. *Washington Cathedral, drawing showing crossing and north transept, c. 1923, by Philip Hubert Frohman (based on Bodley & Vaughan's preliminary design as developed by Frohman, Robb & Little).*

Robb and Philip Frohman about 1923 (Figs. 68, 69). Although these were undoubtedly intended for public presentation and fund-raising rather than as working drawings, they do provide insight into the sort of structure that Bodley and Vaughan envisioned. If one English model for the drawings can be pointed to, it might be Lincoln, for the nave elevation is divided equally between the nave arcade and the triforium-clerestory levels. Both the triforium tracery and that of the main windows is of the curvilinear Decorated style. The vault ribs spring from the colonettes at the base of the clerestory to span the nave with five ribs per bay (there are no subsidiary or lierne ribs). While both Vaughan's and Robb's drawings of the nave show a rather dark interior, they also show a sure knowledge of English precedents presented with a pervading sense of mystery. If finished according to Bodley and Vaughan's plans, Washing-

 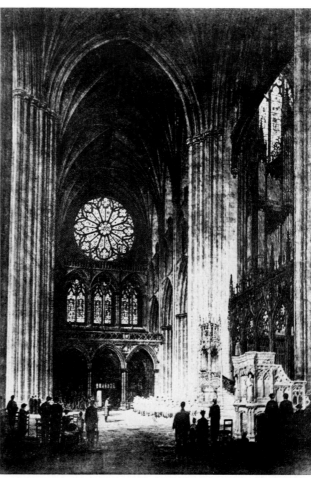

ton Cathedral would have been not only the architect's greatest monument, but also it would have superceded John Loughborough Pearson's Truro Cathedral in Cornwall (1879–1910) as the last cathedral in the nineteenth-century English Gothic Revival style.

When the firm of Frohman, Robb & Little succeeded Vaughan as architects of the cathedral in 1921, Philip Hubert Frohman set about revising the west front. He also raised the height of the central tower from 258 to 330 feet (as well as extended the buttresses out from the lower aisle wall), and made major changes in the nave. While Frohman always maintained that the basic aspects of the original plans were "above criticism,"[35] he devoted half a century to revising and refining the plans, so that, when completed, Washington Cathedral would be mostly his monument.[36]

70. *Washington Cathedral, aerial view (photographed 1981).*

Frohman's cathedral (Fig. 70) is more of an academic exercise in Gothic than that envisioned by Bodley and Vaughan. And it lacks the freshness and originality of the Englishmen's design. For example, Bodley had insisted that the cathedral be constructed of a red stone (such as Lake Superior sandstone), and when Satterlee objected to this, Vaughan then

82

suggested an English stone and strongly advised against any "white stone" (like the Indiana limestone that was finally used).[37] Although Vaughan bowed to Satterlee's wishes on the masonry, a red stone (like that used at Hoar Cross) might have contributed the three-dimensional quality lacking in the drawings and would have provided a textural warmth absent in the present structure.

Although death was to rob Vaughan of the chance to develop fully his and Bodley's original plans, two sections of the cathedral, the sanctuary and the choir, as well as the chapel beneath them, are his designs.[38] Not included in the preliminary plans, the Bethlehem Chapel of the Nativity, begun in 1910 and completed in 1912 (Fig. 71), was designed by Vaughan as the final resting place of Bishop Satterlee, who died in 1908 and who had had the original idea for the chapel.

71. Washington Cathedral, Bethlehem Chapel, 1910–1912.

Echoing the polygonal shape of the apse above it, Bethlehem Chapel is composed of a five-bay nave with three aisles, plus apse, and is spanned by quadripartite vaults which spring from plain, circular piers (Fig. 72). Early Decorated Gothic was chosen after Norman was rejected on the grounds of incongruity with the Gothic exterior. Frohman visited the

72. Washington Cathedral, apse from the east (photographed c. 1921).

73. *Washington Cathedral, apse; choir and crossing under construction, 1927.*

chapel in 1914 and declared Vaughan's crypt more beautiful than he'd seen abroad and called it "the most satisfying example of church architecture in America."[39]

Contrasting with the simplicity of the nave is the richly decorated chancel (with its carved retable, reredos, and fishnet tracery) that fills the arch demarcating nave from apse. Behind the altar is the tomb of Bishop Satterlee, with the recumbent effigy carved by W. D. Caroe, resident architect of Canterbury Cathedral. The apse is lit by five windows created by Kempe's chief designer, John Lisle.

Not wishing to diminish the amount of light entering the chapel, Vaughan altered the cathedral's east end by omitting the ambulatory originally planned for the sanctuary, thereby creating the unusual feature of completely freestanding buttresses (Figs. 72, 73). Begun in 1915 and finished in 1918, the sanctuary was the only portion of the original design that Vaughan built. This small segment of a great whole (with its highly placed windows) shows Vaughan's abiding interest in a sense of wall, while its exposed buttresses show his ability to design in larger forms. But the architectural promise suggested by Bethlehem Chapel and the unique treatment of the apse was not to be realized.[40]

85

The construction of the sanctuary was to have begun in 1914, but, as Vaughan wrote to Bishop Alfred G. Harding, Satterlee's successor, "unfortunately I cannot at present give my entire time to it as I have the three Chapels for the Cathedral of St. John the Divine on hand."[41] In fact, Vaughan did these chapels plus the pulpit and font for what was surely the most impressive ecclesiastical structure of its time.

The result of a much-publicized competition, the winning design for St. John by Heins & La Farge had been under construction for a decade and a half when George L. Heins died in 1907. Although the surviving partner, Grant La Farge, was the actual designer, the construction of St. John had been so marred by structural problems, design changes, and personality conflicts, that the chapter was anxious to engage a new architect. The trustees, reflecting changes in architectural taste (and, no doubt, noting the designs for Washington Cathedral), also believed that Gothic would be more suitable for an Anglican cathedral than La Farge's Byzantine-Romanesque design. In April 1911, La Farge was dismissed and replaced by the consulting architect for St. John, Ralph Adams Cram.[42]

However, the selection of Cram as La Farge's successor was by no means certain. In fact, there is reason to believe that Vaughan was the first choice as architect to complete the project.[43] Although it is not known if the offer was actually made, it is generally believed that Vaughan could have had the commission had he wanted it.[44] Lloyd Hendrick recalled that the architectural gossip of the time was that Vaughan was offered the commission to complete St. John, but refused on the grounds that one cathedral (Washington) was enough for one man.[45] Vaughan's presumed refusal to finish the world's largest cathedral demonstrated a remarkable sense of modesty, but that the opportunity was proferred clearly showed the very high regard in which Vaughan was held.

It is futile to speculate on what Vaughan might have done with St. John the Divine, especially as the cathedral's structural and design problems were such that they are still unresolved. Had Vaughan been forced to wrestle with the problem of unstable foundations or how to span the immense crossing safely, yet imaginatively, his few remaining years would have been fruitlessly spent. As it was, he produced three apsidal chapels for the cathedral that were, according to Cram, "as fine in their grave English way as anything he ever did."[46]

Of the seven apsidal chapels at St. John, the two large ones flanking the choir, St. James (1916) and St. Ansgar (completed in 1918), one of the smaller ones, St. Boniface (1916), were designed by Vaughan (Figs. 74, 75). All are similar to Bethlehem Chapel in that they are pure

74. *Cathedral of St. John the Divine, Chapel of St. James, New York City, 1916.*

English Gothic in the style of the fourteenth century,[47] and have the same form of ribbed vaulting, although the New York chapels have taller proportions and receive more light. All are of Indiana limestone, all have the same form of screen reredos, and two have Kempe glass.

87

75. Cathedral of St. John the Divine, Chapel of St. Ansgar, 1918.

The three chapels at St. John the Divine are Vaughan's last designs and they should be seen as a continuation of his work at Washington. They are similar in detail, historical precedent, and workmanship to Bethlehem Chapel. In their academic use of fourteenth-century detail, these chapels exhibit some of the coldness of the then flourishing Modern Gothic (and perhaps of a 70-year-old bachelor architect), yet they also recall Bodley's suave interior at Hoar Cross. But it is impossible to deny the success of their overall medieval quality and religious effect. Like flawless gems grafted onto the imperfect mass of the cathedral itself, these chapels are of a scale with which Vaughan was comfortable, and as creations in limited and restricted space, they are masterful.

4

OXBRIDGE REVISITED: SCHOOL AND COLLEGE BUILDINGS

. . . the first artistic debate shall be "This House is of the opinion that the nineteenth century Gothicist revival may be justified by the school buildings."

Evelyn Waugh[1]

HENRY VAUGHAN'S original contribution to the history of American architecture is found in his parish churches and especially his designs for schools and colleges. While Vaughan's appointment as architect of Washington Cathedral might be considered the climax of his career, the Chapel of Saint Peter and Saint Paul for St. Paul's School begun twenty years earlier (Fig. 76) is Vaughan's masterpiece.[2]

Had Vaughan died at, say, age fifty and had not lived to design many of his churches or Washington Cathedral, his place in the Gothic Revival in America would still be secure. John Coolidge rightly claims that St. Paul's was the "first American chapel," and the design which initiated a long series of school and college chapels which form the "most successful class of buildings of the Modern Gothic."[3] This chapel was the building that, more than any other, Cram credited with providing the "inspiration to young architects who were working toward a more sincere and expressive manner of building."[4] Only four years after he designed the reliquary-like chapel for the Sisters of St. Margaret, and less than a decade after the completion of Richardson's landmark Trinity Church, Vaughan's St. Paul's appeared upon the American architectural scene as a full-blown English collegiate chapel.[5]

The chapel at St. Paul's was the crowning achievement of the headmastership of Dr. Henry Augustus Coit, "an austere, medieval saint of a

89

man," and, not coincidentally, a strong supporter of the Cowley Fathers in America and a friend of Charles Grafton, Rector of the Church of the Advent.[6] Although founded in 1856, St. Paul's school flourished after the Civil War as one of the most fashionable schools for the preparation of America's new aristocracy of wealth. Just as the Astors, Vanderbilts, and Belmonts housed themselves in French chateaux and Italian Renaissance palazzi in New York, and at watering places like Newport, it was appropriate that they should emulate the English "public" school in the education of their sons. Thus schools like St. Paul's, Groton, and St. Mark's represented an attempt to recreate such upper-class institutions as Eton, Harrow, and Winchester on American soil.[7]

76. Chapel of St. Peter and St. Paul, St. Paul's School, Concord, New Hampshire, 1886–1894.

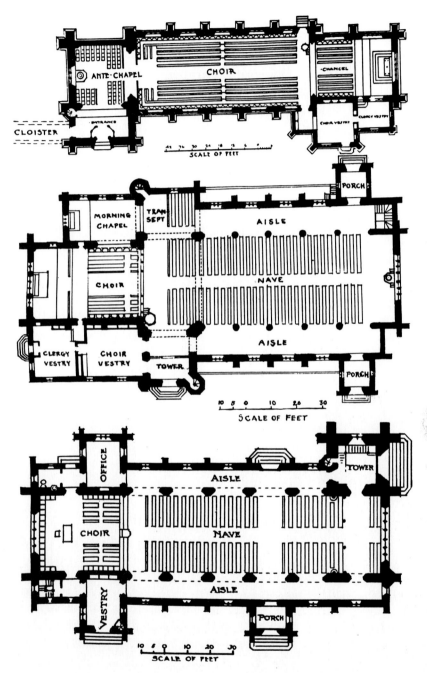

77. St. Paul's School Chapel, plan (top); Christ Church, New Haven, and Western Reserve University Chapel, plans (bottom).

91

Architecture was essential in reinforcing the impression of a school's Englishness, and the Rector of Groton (for whom Vaughan designed two chapels), spoke of the "almighty wall," a phrase borrowed from Edward Thring, headmaster of Uppingham, meaning that "to have a good school a man had to have good buildings."[8] This was affirmed by Bishop Lawrence, who said that the chapels at St. Paul's and Groton "express in a more formal and academic manner the Christian culture of the English speaking people . . . each is chaste, strong, and uplifting."[9]

As a church school, St. Paul's did have a chapel (built in 1858–1860 by the Boston architect George Snell), but by the 1880s the increase in enrollment had rendered it inadequate, and in 1882 a list headed by Mr. Stevens of Hoboken, New Jersey with a subscription of $10,000 was in circulation.[10] By 1884 the building fund had reached $51,000, about half the amount needed, and construction commenced with the laying of the cornerstone on St. Matthew's Day, September 21, 1886.[11] The chapel was completed (except for the upper half of the tower) and consecrated on June 5, 1888; the tower was finished in 1894.

In its long, narrow plan (Fig. 77), with antechapel, nave (referred to by the school as the choir), chancel, and vestries, St. Paul's clearly evokes the spirit of Oxford and Cambridge. But while the chapel marks

78. Bodley & Garner, Queens' College Chapel, Cambridge, 1890–1891.

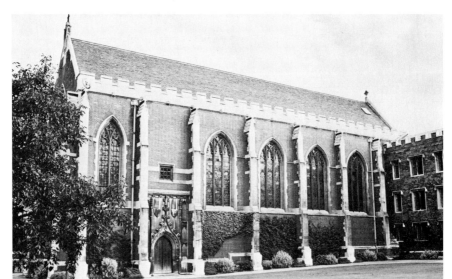

79. St. Cuthbert's Church, Wells, Somerset, 13th–15th centuries.

a scholarly return to the Middle Ages (especially when compared to the American Gothic Revival churches that preceded it), it is closest to Bodley's chapel at Queens' College, Cambridge (1890–1891). The chapel at Queens' College (Fig. 78) lacks a western tower, but the proportions of the red brick nave with its highly placed windows and simple forms are too similar to Vaughan's chapel to be ignored. Bodley's chapel has the "in choir" seating (the pews and stalls, placed parallel to the side walls, face each other across the aisle) that was so novel in America when Vaughan employed it at St. Paul's.[12]

As in other Vaughan churches, the windows of St. Paul's are both small in relation to the space around them and placed fairly high with unbroken wall beneath them; this window-wall composition acts as a unifying element, rather than detracting from the elaborate tracery. The

93

steep but unbroken roof (without the iron cresting or polychromatic slate so prevalent at this time) also contributes to the remarkably harmonious and superbly proportioned body of the chapel. The whole structure gives the impression of verticality and height so often lacking in earlier American churches, and the handling of the brick surfaces gives a warmth suggestive of the country houses of Sir Edwin Lutyens.[13]

Vaughan's tower for St. Paul's (Fig. 81) was something entirely different from the brooch spires of Pugin, Street, or Pearson. When completed in 1894, the tower represented one of the finest recreations of the magnificent fifteenth-century Perpendicular towers of the West Country. It recalls such Somerset examples as the tower of St. Mary the Virgin,

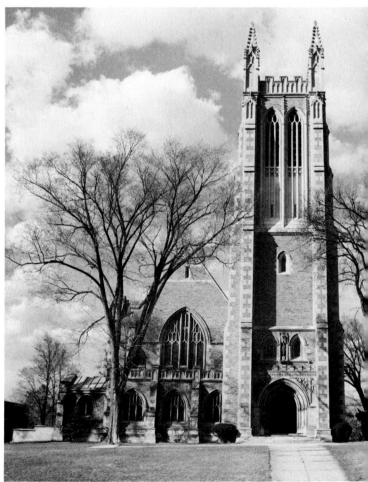

80. Allen & Collens, Thompson Memorial Chapel, Williams College, Williamstown, Massachusetts, 1903–1905.

81. *St. Paul's School Chapel, extension of the chancel, 1928.*

Huish Episcopi, and more especially, that of the less elaborate St. Cuthbert in Wells (Fig. 79), not to mention Merton College Chapel at Oxford. Like its English antecedents, Vaughan's tower was never designed for a spire; it is the full width of the chapel itself, and (like the tower of St. Cuthbert) it is composed of only a belfry stage with two long windows on each side. In contrast to the plain walls of the rest of the building, all of the chapel's rich decoration seems to be concentrated on the tower parapet.

It was the Perpendicular tower, based on the most glorious phase of English art, that so appealed to Cram and other architects of his generation. From St. Paul's onward, the square, spireless tower became one of the characteristic forms of the Modern Gothic style, and it is easy to recognize St. Paul's as the progenitor of such collegiate chapel towers as the one at Williams College by Allen & Collens or at Cram's St. George's School in Newport (Figs. 80, 134).

When completed, the tower of St. Paul's was almost as tall (120 feet) as the chapel was long. In 1927–1928 the impressive quality of this proportional relationship was diminished when Cram's office (under the direction of Frank E. Cleveland) doubled the length of the chancel by cutting it, moving the sanctuary eastward, and inserting two new bays

95

82. *St. Paul's School Chapel, cloister connecting the chapel with the Study at left (drawing published in 1890).*

83. *St. Paul's School Chapel from the southeast, before enlargement; the Study, the Annex, and Goodhue's cloister to the left.*

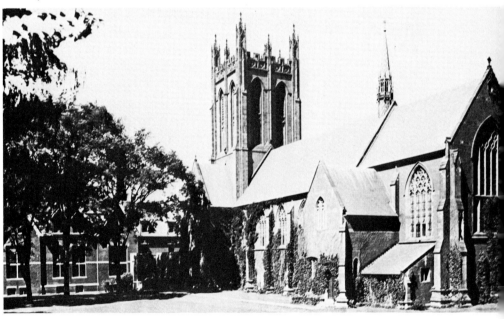

84. St. Paul's School Chapel, interior before enlargement.

85. St. Paul's School Chapel, interior.

(Fig. 81).[14] In 1920 Bertram Goodhue designed a cloister which extended four bays from the west front and abruptly stopped. Goodhue's slype replaced Vaughan's earlier, timber-framed cloister which connected the chapel with a neighboring building called the Study (Figs. 82, 83).[15]

Despite the decidedly English character of the brick exterior, with its Springfield sandstone trim, it is the interior of St. Paul's (Figs. 84, 85) with its tall proportions (the choir is 31 by 78 feet and 48 feet high; before its extension the chancel was 25 by 35 and 49 feet high), wood ceiling, English glass, rich oak carving, and numerous memorials that gives the impression that this *is* an English college chapel.[16] The interior of St. Paul's was as influential as the exterior, for it demonstrated that an historically correct Gothic church need not be picturesque and gloomy. Rather, the interior of St. Paul's bespeaks height, lightness, and dignity, as well as what Coolidge describes as an "atmosphere of suave self-respect, of pious idealism tempered with common-sense."[17]

The oak ceiling of the five-bay choir at St. Paul's is set off by arched trusses springing from slender stone shafts. The bays are divided into square panels by molded ribs and have carved bosses at the intersections. The cornice line of the west screen is carried around the choir walls to define the back of the stalls. The long pews are progressively raised toward the wall. There are five windows per side, all framed by stone arches; the walls are plain.[18]

The chancel is set off from the choir by an unobtrusive chancel arch, but the chancel seats and canopies pick up and continue the lines of those in the choir. The organ (Fig. 86), originally a Hutchings, is located in the first bay of the south wall.[19] The fourth bay (one of the original two bays) contains the sanctuary, with its sumptuous wood carving and floor of Belgian Black and Ceneri marble. Bela Pratt's 1898 effigy of Dr. Coit in Carrara marble is set in the north wall under a canopy which calls to mind such English medieval burial monuments as the Percy tomb in Beverley Minster and those designed by Bodley at Ely, Lincoln, and Winchester. The chancel is spanned by quadripartite vaults which spring from slender colonettes.

The focus of such a funnel-like interior is naturally the east end, and Vaughan provided the fitting climax with a simple altar, a large reredos, and a Decorated east window. Covering almost half of the wall, the reredos (designed in 1894) is based on an obvious English example (in this case Winchester Cathedral)—a type practically unknown in America at the time. As on the tiered facades of Lichfield, Wells, or Lincoln cathedrals, there is a gallery of six early saints and churchmen (including

86. St. Paul's School Chapel, organ.

William of Wykeham holding a model of this chapel) flanking the enthroned Christ, as well as two paintings representing the Transfiguration and the Resurrection. The lower level has five similar paintings, illustrating scenes from the life of Christ, grouped around the painted altarpiece of the Adoration of the Magi. The carving was done by Johannes Kirchmayer—and is considered his masterpiece—while the paintings are by Clayton & Bell (who also did much of the stained glass). The reredos would reappear at Christ Church, New Haven and at Washington, but Cram considered that at St. Paul's as "undoubtedly the finest" of its type.[20]

Vaughan's detailing is a combination of scholarly historicism and a Victorian Arts and Crafts sensibility—that is, it is eclectic in its sources but contemporary in its technique and execution. The carving throughout the chapel, like that of the reredos, is competently designed, well executed, and extremely rich, but it is rather more archaeological than inventive. This derivative aspect is particularly evident in the window tracery, which is often little more than a reworking of an English precedent. The curvilinear tracery at St. Paul's, for example, is modeled on similar window compositions at Wells Cathedral.[21] However, Vaughan's reliance on Decorated sources constituted an innovation in America, where few Gothic Revival architects had either Vaughan's knowledge of English architecture or his mastery of such detailing.

From an architectural standpoint, the romantic but restrained exterior is perhaps a finer piece of work, although it is the interior of St. Paul's that comes closest to the drama of Bodley's Church of the Holy Angels at Hoar Cross. Besides its importance as one of the landmarks of the Gothic Revival in America, St. Paul's impresses the visitor as a symbol of the essence of academic tradition and English culture—it is both theatrical and reverential.

Although St. Paul's was undoubtedly the most important building in Vaughan's career, it was only the first of a number of projects that he undertook for Dr. Coit and subsequent rectors. In fact, from the beginning of the chapel until about 1902 Vaughan was considered the official school architect.

In 1895 Vaughan made plans for a building that would include a library, auditorium, and choir room, to be erected at an estimated cost of $75,000, but the project was abandoned when funds were not forthcoming.[22] Vaughan built the Annex in 1898, a simple, four-story brick schoolhouse attached to a larger structure called the Study. This complex (Fig. 83), which is no longer extant, was attached to the chapel first by

Vaughan's cloister and later by Goodhue's. Vaughan also built two large brick dormitories at St. Paul's, the Lower School and the New Upper School.

The Lower School (a dormitory for seventh- and eighth-grade boys) was begun in 1890 and completed in the winter of 1891–1892, at a cost of $114,544.[23] A drawing of the dormitory which was published in the *American Architect and Building News* in February 1891 listed the architects as Vaughan and Henry Paston Clark. Clark, a graduate of the Massachusetts Institute of Technology and the Ecole des Beaux Arts, had his office at 5 Pemberton Square, as did Vaughan, from 1889 to 1891. But, as the dormitory's design followed the style of "English school buildings of the eighteenth century," there is little doubt that the primary inspiration for the Lower School was Vaughan's (Fig. 87).[24]

Not unlike certain early academic buildings in Colonial America, the brick Lower School had pedimented dormers, projecting pavilions, and pedimented gable ends. But in spite of these elements, the three wings of varying lengths which intersect the main block are hardly symmetrical, and the tall proportions and the tower with cupola (which ingeniously contained a fire escape) are more medieval than Georgian in spirit. The doorway in the drawing is flanked by paired pilasters with

87. St. Paul's School, Lower School, 1890–1892.

88. Bodley & Garner, River House, London, 1879.

full entablature below a window with Baroque scrolls, and is reminiscent of some of the neoclassical decoration applied to buildings in early seventeenth-century England. However, the source for the Lower School is also found in such works by Bodley as River House, built along the Chelsea Embankment in 1879 (Fig. 88). River House has the same tall proportions as the Lower School, and the style of both buildings is a rather free interpretation of the early Georgian style known as Anglo-Dutch.[25]

The sources for Vaughan's last work at St. Paul's School are less obscure, but also owe a great deal to his association with Bodley & Garner, particularly their design of St. Swithun's Quadrangle at Magdalen College. The New Upper School (1902–1904, Fig. 89) is a large, four-story structure, its U-shaped plan forming three sides of a quadrangle. The brick walls of the New Upper School feature white belt courses and quoins, oriel windows, and a ground-level cloister across the central section (similar to the arcade at Good Shepherd parish house of the same year). The north wing, a monumental block divided into buttressed bays with tiered lancets and a large "east window," is the refectory. While the style of the dormitory part of the building is Jacobean, the dining hall is late Gothic and looks like the chapel of an English college.

89. St. Paul's School, New Upper School, 1902–1904.

90. *New Upper School, refectory.*

The interior (Fig. 90) is a great open hall in the manner of the great halls at Oxford and Cambridge. Above the oak-paneled walls (lined with portraits of school rectors and masters) is an elaborate timber-framed ceiling similar to that at St. Mary's, Dorchester. The east wall features a large stained-glass window by Kempe depicting such English divines as Sir Thomas More, William of Wykeham, and Roger Bacon.

The New Upper School was not as successful as the chapel was, and residents were quick to point out that the architect had neglected to provide closets. More damning, the cost of the dormitory "was so great as to seriously embarrass the school."[26] But if it was a practical failure, aesthetically the New Upper School reflected Vaughan's high standards. Although based on a late Gothic style (when it was showing the effects of the Renaissance), the New Upper School is, in its quiet and unassum-

91. Mary Frances Searles Science Building, Bowdoin College, Brunswick, Maine, 1894.

ing way, just as evocative of Oxford and Cambridge as the more familiar Gothic of Princeton and Yale.

Situated between the Lower and the New Upper Schools, both stylistically and chronologically, was the Searles Science building for Bowdoin College in Brunswick, Maine (Fig. 91). A far more successful academic work than either of the dormitories, Searles was begun in 1893 and completed in 1894 at a cost of $143,000.[27] Providing much-needed facilities for the departments of physics, biology, and chemistry, Searles Hall was donated by Edward F. Searles in memory of his wife, Mary Frances.[28]

In his "Address of Acceptance," Bowdoin President William DeWitt Hyde mentioned that the building's internal arrangement was the result of cooperation between the various science professors and the architect,

92. *Bodley & Garner, Master's Lodgings, University College, Oxford, 1879.*

but that the material, color, and proportions of the building were determined by the donor.[29] Hyde's references to the taste of Mr. Searles aside, the U-shaped, three-story hall with its Flemish gables, towers, and cupola is typical of Vaughan's work. For a probable source for Searles Hall (labeled by the college as "Elizabethan"), one need only look as far back as 1879 and Garner's Master's Lodgings at University College, Oxford (Fig. 92), or his re-creation of an Elizabethan prodigy house, Hewell Grange, Worcestershire (1884–1891, Fig. 93), not to mention River House.

A large building (172 feet long with 107-foot wings) built of brick with buff-colored Amherst sandstone trim, Searles Hall's dominant emphasis is vertical. As a continuation of the academic style Vaughan initiated with the Lower School at St. Paul's, the science building at Bowdoin is one of the earliest scholarly revivals of Jacobean in this country, and is thus the ancestor of countless Jacobean school buildings across the United States.

Despite the need to provide a good deal of natural light in an essentially utilitarian structure, Vaughan did not allow the abundant fenestration to sublimate his love of wall, the textural surfaces of which are subtly emphasized by the stone trim.[30] At the same time, Vaughan's delight in detail found expression in the medallions—bearing telescopes, geological hammers, and other scientific iconography—which adorn the Flemish gables.

Vaughan was awarded an honorary Master of Arts degree at the 1894 Bowdoin commencement (along with Charles McKim, who designed the school's neoclassical art museum), and the trustees and overseers of

93. Bodley & Garner, Hewell Grange, Worcestershire, 1884–1889.

the college further voted to present Vaughan with an embossed parchment expressing

their high appreciation of the fitness and excellence of his work as architect of the Mary F. Searles Science Building. With true art he has clothed with dignity and beauty a structure admirably adapted to the practical purposes which it is to serve.[31]

While the requirements of scientific education have changed since the 1890s (the inscription over the main entrance reads: "Nature's laws are God's thoughts"), Searles Hall is one of Vaughan's least dated and most satisfying academic structures.

Vaughan designed another large building for Bowdoin, the Hubbard Library, completed in 1903 (Fig. 94). This was the gift of Thomas

94. Hubbard Library, Bowdoin College, 1902–1903.

95. *Hubbard Grand Stand, Bowdoin College, 1903.*

Hubbard, the man who had been so instrumental in persuading Searles to donate the science building to the college. Bowdoin had desperately needed new library facilities for a long time, but never had the funds or alumni wealthy enough to provide them. General Hubbard, however, was an exception, and in 1900 he offered an endowed library "to be constructed to please the eye" and without regard to cost.[32] Even before the gift was publicly announced, Hubbard wrote to Vaughan asking him to draw up plans.[33] Vaughan was obviously the ideal architect for Hubbard, who had specific ideas regarding every detail of the new library. When completed, the final cost of the building was nearly double the originally proposed sum of $150,000. During construction of the Bowdoin Library, General Hubbard also donated a small stadium to the college (Fig. 95).[34]

Hubbard Hall (which sits at the south end of the Bowdoin common, near Searles Hall, McKim's Renaissance art museum, and Richard Upjohn's Romanesque chapel) is a large T-shaped structure built of red brick, Indiana limestone, and Maine granite.[35] The main portion is 46 by 176 feet with a 100-foot tower; the rear wing is 90 feet long. This rear section (the stack area) is a somewhat awkward pile with strips of stone-trimmed windows running up six narrow floors into the peaked gables. The main block does not have as much light-colored stone intruding on Vaughan's

109

beloved brick surfaces. The end walls, for example, have only simple quoins and occasional belt courses (like those at Good Shepherd). The main facade is dominated by the tower, which is framed by a sloping slate roof almost as tall as the two floors it shelters. Two projecting pavilions with full-height Jacobean oriels pick up the rhythm of the tower.

Vaughan described the style of Hubbard as "17th century Gothic . . . the last stage of Gothic in England . . . followed by the Renaissance. Many of the College buildings of Oxford and Cambridge are in this composite style."[36] Predictably, the source for Hubbard can be found in England, in this case at Magdalen College, Oxford: not the well-known early sixteenth-century tower that is usually cited (and that Vaughan used for Christ Church, New Haven), but instead the tower and buildings of Bodley & Garner's St. Swithun's Quadrangle (Fig. 96).[37] Hubbard Hall is by no means an exact copy (the Oxford model is stone, while some details come from the Master's House at University College), but the tower is almost identical to that in Garner's competition drawing for St.

96. Bodley & Garner, St. Swithun's Quadrangle, Magdalen College, Oxford, 1880.

97. Groton Chapel from the east.

Swithun's. Garner's drawing has the "flying ribbon" titles so characteristic of Pugin and one of them appears in stone over the main entrance to Hubbard Library bearing the inscription: "Here Seek Converse with the Wise of All Ages."

In describing both Searles and Hubbard halls, Montgomery Schuyler, the leading architectural critic of the late nineteenth century, recalled the "pranks the English architects were playing at Oxford and Cambridge during the Jacobean and Caroline periods," but added that Hubbard is "a dignified, scholarly and appropriate performance that does not misbecome the traditions of Magdalen and Merton."[38] Just as Vaughan's nearby St. Andrew's Church employed late Gothic that, in spite of its very Englishness, seemed happily suited to late nineteenth-century New England, Searles and Hubbard halls are quite at home in their American collegiate setting.

As important as Searles and Hubbard halls are in the revival of the last phases of English Gothic, it is another school chapel, St. John's at the Groton School (Figs. 1, 97), that constitutes Vaughan's great collegiate work after St. Paul's. Groton is similar to St. Paul's in that both

111

institutions were modeled on the English public school and drew their support from America's financial and social establishment (for example, J. P. Morgan helped found Groton and served on its board of trustees). Begun in 1899 and consecrated in the autumn of 1900, Groton Chapel was the gift of William Amory Gardner, a wealthy Bostonian, a parishioner at the Church of the Advent, and one of Groton's three founding masters. Gardner had given an earlier chapel to Groton in 1887 which was also by Vaughan.[39]

The style of the new chapel at Groton was the topic of considerable discussion, in view of the strong opinion of some that it should be a "New England meeting house" of brick to harmonize with the existing buildings by Peabody & Stearns. However, Rector Endicott Peabody believed that the chapel should be primarily an inspirational symbol of the school and nothing less than "one of the most beautiful ecclesiastical structures in America."[40]

Groton Chapel is a rather compact, even taut design, especially in comparison with the spread-out plan of St. Paul's. Here Vaughan's most elaborate tower is attached to an extremely simple plan, the chapel being a severe, elongated rectangle broken only by the tower and a small sacristy. The chapel's boxlike configuration and its roofline bring to mind such Tudor buildings as King's College Chapel, Cambridge, or the chapel at Eton. Although Vaughan had used Perpendicular details on his church interiors, and a Perpendicular tower at St. Paul's, all of Groton is in the Perpendicular style.

The limestone employed for the Groton Chapel imparts a dry, almost brittle quality in strong sunlight that seems at odds with Vaughan's usual delight in warm materials. Compared with the heavy masonry of St. Barnabas or the patined brick of St. Paul's, the walls of Groton Chapel seem flatter, almost as if the stone were but a thin membrane. Perhaps Vaughan had in mind the harsh effect of this light-colored masonry at Groton when he argued against its use for Washington Cathedral.

Furthermore, the decoration gives the effect of being applied to Groton's plain masses, creating a thinness and attenuation of details that is in keeping with its Perpendicular models. The windows, for example, show the flat and rectilinear qualities so characteristic of much late English Gothic tracery. In spite of its somewhat confectionary appearance, the tower detailing clearly shows Vaughan's mastery of the Perpendicular vocabulary. With its triple recesses, quatrefoils, gargoyles, and open, stepped battlements, the Groton tower is the best example of the Perpendicular style in the United States.

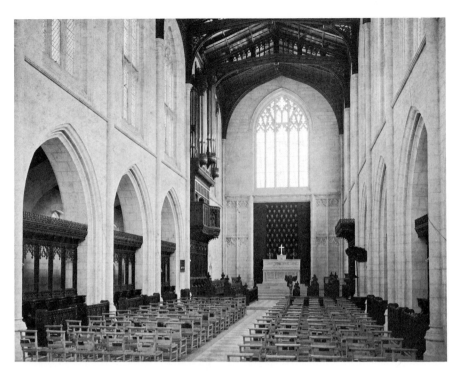

98. *Groton Chapel, interior (before installation of the stained glass).*

If the exterior of Groton seems restrained and overly linear, the same may be said of the interior (Figs. 2, 98), for the unrelieved configuration of the outside is repeated. The effect verges on the Spartan, but is in keeping with Peabody's concept of a boys' school, as well as his low churchmanship.[41] In short, Groton is a collegiate chapel (like King's Chapel or Bodley's Queens' College Chapel) in that there is no break in ceiling or walls to differentiate choir and chancel. The choir does have stalls placed opposite each other, but these are only a single step higher than the chairs for the congregants. All the elements in the tall, narrow chapel combine to give a feeling of flatness, which is accentuated by the smooth stonework. The wall holding the large west window is absolutely plain, while the east wall is relieved only by four panels flanking the dossal that serves as a backdrop to the simple marble altar. (An elaborate reredos was designed but never built.) The verticality of the chapel is further stressed by single, uninterrupted colonettes that run between the bay arches up to the springing of the roof trusses, just below the ceiling. The low-pitched ceiling is composed of quartered panels supported by trusses pierced with thin lancet cutouts. Modeled on the fifteenth-century wooden roofs that so enrich West Country parish churches and are found

113

in the "wool churches" of East Anglia, this splendid ceiling makes up for the lack of ornament elsewhere.[42] The donor of the chapel remarked that the windows (all by Kempe, except for one by Clayton & Bell), as well as the "high roof and honesty of ornamentation," produce a "prevailing note of serenity," and that "age and association will make it very dear to Grotonians."[43]

The Groton Chapel inevitably invites comparison with the chapel at St. Paul's School. Although not as elaborately furnished nor as warm as St. Paul's, Groton is just as effective. Groton has not been altered or enlarged by other architects, and, as a pure example of its style, it has a unity and homogeneity lacking at St. Paul's. Certainly Groton furthered the fashion for Perpendicular collegiate buildings (although its crisp economy of form and detail was more easily emulated by later Gothicists, who often subverted its virtues into a kind of sterile dryness). And, like St. Paul's, Groton is a milestone in Vaughan's career as well as being one of America's major neo-Gothic monuments.

99. *Amasa Stone*
Memorial Chapel, Western
Reserve University,
Cleveland, Ohio, 1909–1911.

The Groton Chapel was visited by Clara Stone Hay (widow of John Hay, former Secretary of State, Ambassador to the Court of St. James, and friend of Henry Adams) and her sister Flora Stone Mather who were searching for an architect to design a chapel for Western Reserve University in Cleveland. These ladies were favorably impressed with Groton, and gave Vaughan the commission for the Amasa Stone Memorial Chapel in honor of their father, a railroad financier who had generously endowed the Ohio university.[44] Constructed in 1909–1910 at a cost of $167,881 and dedicated in 1911, Stone Chapel (Figs. 99, 100) was one of Vaughan's most ambitious projects of the Washington Cathedral period.[45]

Stone Chapel "will remind you immediately," as a Cleveland newspaper noted, "of that at St. Paul's School," but it also has the same open plan and narrow side aisles as the Church of the Redeemer, as well as the corner tower at the west end (Fig. 39).[46] This Bodlean block is closest to

100. Western Reserve Chapel, interior.

Groton, for here, too, Vaughan articulated the side aisles externally and built flying buttresses, a feature that Vaughan was working on at Washington Cathedral.[47] This is also one of the few buildings described by the architect in anything more than sketchy terms:

The style of architecture is late Decorated Gothic. The material used for all the exterior walls and for much of the interior is fine cut Indiana limestone. The plan of the chapel consists of nave and choir of the same width and height, with narrow side aisles, which carries the arched trusses of the barrel vaulted ceiling. The nave is seated to accommodate five hundred and forty-five students . . . there is a small west end gallery for visitors which will seat about seventy persons . . . the fittings have all been specially designed and are of oak, stained a dark color. The organ was made by the Austin Organ Company. . . . It is placed in the choir above the stalls and has a richly carved oak case. The nave is well lighted by clerestory windows, and by large west and east windows. The east window has been filled with magnificent stained glass representing the crucifixion, designed and made by C. E. Kempe and Company, of London. . . . The entire length of the chapel is one hundred and forty-five feet, six inches, not including the projections of the buttresses. The width of the nave and aisles is fifty-three feet, three inches; the height from floor to cornice is thirty-nine feet, and the apex of the ceiling fifty-two feet. The tower is twenty-four feet square and one hundred and twenty feet to the top of the corner pinnacles. A chime or peal of bells will eventually be placed in the tower.[48]

Despite some minor problems with lighting and acoustics, Stone Chapel was generally regarded as a laudable success; it provided a suitable impression of collegiate respectability with suggestions of the academic past of the great English universities.[49] The tower and west end were directly inspired by the similar arrangement at Groton (as are the east and west windows). The tower, however, is modeled on the chapel tower at St. Paul's School, but here the lack of the warm texture of brick is compensated for by an increase in decorative detail. The entrance window has reticulated tracery, shields similar to those employed at Hubbard Library and the Church of the Redeemer are found above the termination points of the buttresses, and the St. Swithun's angel adorns the parapet on three sides (the north parapet displays a gargoyle in keeping with traditional medieval practice). The Stone Chapel tower is even closer to St. Cuthbert's, Wells, than is the tower at St. Paul's, while the proportions are more attenuated. The cathedral-like Bodlean interior is one of the most handsome evocations of an English collegiate chapel in America, and it demonstrates that Vaughan's Anglo-Catholic style could be successfully adapted for non-Episcopalian worship.

116

5

THE LEGACY OF JONES AND WREN: NON-GOTHIC WORK

There are those who would like to see a restoration of some precious monument of antiquity of the Middle Ages. . . . Henry Vaughan is a true artist and therefore never willing to copy . . . never willing to sacrifice purpose to appearance.

Reverend John Mitchell Page, *Holy Cross Magazine,* February 1903

HENRY VAUGHAN, while known primarily for his work in English Gothic, claimed to be able to design in the "Elizabethan, Palladian, Italian, Renaissance, Medieval, Baronial, Romanesque, or Colonial" styles.[1] This is hardly a surprising claim coming from an architect working in the golden age of eclecticism, but it should be understood that he meant those styles as interpreted by English designers—he was referring to William Kent, Inigo Jones, and Sir Christopher Wren, rather than to Palladio, Alberti, and Vignola. He relied upon his knowledge of British architecture from the Middle Ages to the Georgian period for appropriate expression, and the same hallmarks of linearity, sense of wall, and refined sensibility are found in all his buildings. Vaughan was a pioneer in the introduction of English neo-Palladian and Georgian forms, much as he was for English Gothic, and although far less known Vaughan's non-Gothic work provides an unexpected dimension to his artistry.

As a member of the tradition of ecclesiologically minded architects, Vaughan generally limited his use of Gothic to appropriate buildings—Decorated and Perpendicular for churches, chapels, and cathedrals, and Elizabethan and Jacobean for schools or academic structures. But just as his first church, St. Andrew's, Newcastle, introduced the hitherto unknown

117

101. Gladisfen, Newcastle, Maine, 1883.

fifteenth-century half-timber mode, Vaughan's early non-Gothic commissions were equally different from the prevailing nonecclesiastical late Victorian styles.

Gladisfen, a house built for William T. Glidden (the donor of St. Andrew's), is probably Vaughan's first work in Georgian (Fig. 101).[2] Coming at a time when Vaughan's Boston contemporaries were taking tentative steps toward an appreciation and revival of the American Colonial style, Gladisfen is a fully developed Georgian-style mansion. Located not far from St. Andrew's, this Newcastle house is a two-story, five-bay, symmetrical composition, complete with a slightly projecting pedimented central pavilion and full-height Ionic pilasters.

118

The sources for Gladisfen can be found in a number of major New England houses of the Middle Georgian period, such as Lady Pepperell ₄ house in Kittery Point, Maine (c. 1760), and particularly the Vassall-Longfellow house in Cambridge, Massachusetts (Fig. 102) of 1759. In fact, Gladisfen is so remarkably like the poet Longfellow's home that Glidden may have expressed a preference for a similar house. The same balustrade crowns the gently pitched roof, identical dormers flank the pediment of the central pavilion, and similar fenestration is evident, with minor differences, such as the circular window in the pediment at Newcastle and Vaughan's somewhat awkward Palladian main doorway. However, only the facade is so particularly "American," for the rest of Gladisfen, especially the interior, is English Palladian in inspiration.

102. Vassall-Longfellow House, Cambridge, Massachusetts, 1759.

In 1886, Vaughan designed a house on Block Island which is thoroughly English and unlike any Georgian house in America. Completed two years later, this Rhode Island summer home was the aptly named Dream House of Vaughan's patron, Edward Searles (Fig. 103).[3] Early photographs of the Searles house show it to have been large (70 by 100 feet), built of white pine and topped by an octagonal dome. While a contemporary newspaper account describes Dream House as being of the "old colonial style," and with a great hall "after the Southern style of architecture," it was clearly like nothing previously seen on American shores.[4] The dome (and the square picture gallery it lighted) calls to mind the one at Castle Howard (1699–1712) by Sir John Vanbrugh, and the total effect recalls English country houses of the Queen Anne period. However, the rusticated *piano nobile* on which the house sits, the ground floor arcading, and the double tetrastyle portico in the center of the main front are clearly neo-Palladian in inspiration. The Searles Mansion is a rare instance of the revival of early eighteenth-century English neoclassical forms and is perhaps the most academic recreation of Palladianism in America since Thomas Jefferson.

*103. Searles Mansion, Block Island, Rhode Island, 1886–1888
(dome was blown off in a hurricane).*

104. Bathhouse, Searles Mansion, Block Island (photograph taken c. 1904).

Vaughan's debt to the English disciples of Andrea Palladio and Inigo Jones is further demonstrated by the bathhouse he erected for Searles (Fig. 104). This structure had a Greek cross plan and featured Palladian vocabulary and a dome on a circular drum. The bathhouse recalls such neo-Palladian garden buildings as Vanbrugh's Belvedere at Castle Howard (1726) and the similar Casina that Sir William Chambers designed for Lord Charlemont at Marino, near Dublin, before 1759.

Vaughan's chief talents did not lie in domestic architecture: The designing of a house with all the personal requirements and specialized spatial demands of the individual client is quite different from amassing a series of historical details into a symbolic ecclesiastical or scholastic composition. Vaughan nevertheless demonstrated his ability to design in a style in which he had no training, for he "was charmed by the New

105. The Thistles, Dublin, New Hampshire, 1888.

England summer houses and wanted to build one," and the Thistles in Dublin, New Hampshire (Fig. 105) is quite unlike either the Maine or Block Island houses.[5]

    The Thistles was begun in 1888 for Mary Bradford Foote, headmistress of a girls' school in Cambridge, Massachusetts. Miss Foote met Vaughan in England and befriended him; their friendship continued when Vaughan came to America, as he was a frequent visitor to the Foote home in Cambridge. Mary Foote decided that her young nephew (for whom she was guardian) needed country air and engaged Vaughan to design a summer cottage in Dublin, an artists' colony and watering place popular with socially prominent Bostonians. Built at a cost of $10,000, the Thistles was ready in time for the Footes and Vaughan to have Christmas dinner there in 1888.[6]

    Not unlike other houses erected at this time in such New England summer resorts as Newport and Bar Harbor (not to mention Dublin itself)[7] by architects like William Ralph Emerson, John Calvin Stevens, Peabody & Stearns, and McKim, Mead & White, the Foote house has many of the features of the Shingle Style: a prominent porch, picturesque massing, abundant dormers, and bay windows, as well as Colonial Revival details such as a Palladian window and a gambrel roof. Despite the obvious similarities with the very American Shingle Style, the somewhat elongated proportions and Queen Anne details must have been inspired by contemporary English architects practicing in the same idiom.[8] Even if Vaughan recognized his limitations as a designer of houses, the Thistles is no mean achievement, and one wonders why its reasonably successful formula was not repeated.

Bodley's pious missionary was perhaps happiest—and at his best—when designing buildings that more directly expressed his religious faith. One Vaughan building that is both Georgian *and* intended for religious purposes is his monastery for the Order of the Holy Cross at West Park, New York (1902–1904, Fig. 106).

106. Holy Cross Monastery, West Park, New York, 1902–1904.

Vaughan was the logical choice to build the monastery, especially in light of the fact that he designed the Holy Cross mission church in New York City. In accepting the commission in 1900, Vaughan noted that the "S. Paul School building has not to be begun before spring" and that he had "nearly completed the working drawings for Bowdoin Coll. Library."[9] Built at a cost of $50,000, Holy Cross Monastery was more satisfactory to its clients than the New Upper School had been.[10] It was

. . . a building unmistakably of today . . . with enough individuality not to be mistaken for a private dwelling, school or a mere institution, although it has points of resemblance to all. Those who would have predicted picturesque extravagance, etc. find a compact and economically planned American edifice. . . . Those who expect a kind of volunteer prison find a home which smiles through open archways, well proportioned doors and windows, and shows them an array of comfortable chimneys, gables, and dormers . . . all queer, picturesque and theatrical expectations have been so successfully disappointed.[11]

Despite such a glowing tribute, there is some indication that the monastery's style was not exactly what Vaughan originally intended—perhaps its very restraint was imposed by Father Sturgis Allen and the Father Superior—but Vaughan reserved the right to use his "own judgment as to the style of architecture."[12] Even this was challenged, and Vaughan was regarded not without some sense of exasperation.[13]

In any case, the first Episcopal monastery in the United States is one of Vaughan's least eclectic buildings. On a bluff overlooking the Hudson River, the "house" is a long, rectangular brick block with pedimented gables at both ends, front and rear, giving the general appearance of an H-plan building seen in elevation. The fenestration is extremely simple, although there is an open arcade on the river side (another instance of the enclosed cloister used at Good Shepherd and the New Upper School). The overall simplicity of the monastery is reflected in the almost Spartan ground-floor chapel. Perhaps closest in style to the early Georgian of the Lower School at St. Paul's School, the importance of Holy Cross is rather more historical than architectural.[14]

The 1891 Lower School served as the initiator of Vaughan's Georgian and institutional buildings in much the same way St. Andrew's, Newcastle, did for his half-timbered village churches. These buildings all have the same flat and linear brick walls, the same tall Wrenian proportions, and similar pediments. Structures like the Searles High School in Great Barrington, Massachusetts (1897–1898), the Study Annex

107. Lawrence Home for Aged People, Lawrence, Massachusetts, 1909–1910.

at St. Paul's School, or the Home for Aged People in Lawrence, Massachusetts, seem to spring from the same sources and show a single-minded approach to a certain type and size of institutional building.

The largest of these, the Lawrence Home of 1910 (Fig. 107), might be mistaken for a Colonial Revival building. Yet the tall proportions of the central and flanking pediments, as well as the flatness and thinness of the walls, looks back not to eighteenth-century American buildings (like the first edifice at Yale or Hollis Hall at Harvard), but to their English sources—to late Wren and the early Georgians.

The direct English derivation (as well as Vaughan's reasons for choosing a non-Gothic style for a Methodist establishment) is even more evident

108. *Lawrence Home, chapel.*

in the small chapel for the Lawrence Home (Fig. 108) . The round barrel vault and the composite columns and pilasters supporting a small gallery appear to be modeled after some of Wren's City churches or his chapel at Pembroke College, Cambridge, of 1663.

The octagonal cupola on the roof of the Lawrence Home appears on a number of Vaughan's non-Gothic works, and, like the consecration crosses on his churches, serves as a kind of signature. Although there are possible American sources for this cupola form in public buildings of the Middle Georgian period (for example, Carpenters' Hall in Philadelphia, 1770–1771), it derives from River House and ultimately from Wren and Sir Roger Pratt. A seventeenth-century version appeared on Searles Hall at Bowdoin, and Vaughan also used it on another stylistically transitional work, the public library in Swansea, Massachusetts, of 1900 (Fig. 109).

The Stevens Public Library is built of granite with red sandstone trim, and, like neighboring Christ Church, was a bequest by Vaughan's friend, Frank S. Stevens. Vaughan described it as

. . . a simple form of Elizabethan—a style which was thought would harmonize best with the Gothic church, and the Romanesque town hall, between which it

109. Frank S. Stevens Public Library, Swansea, Massachusetts, 1900.

110. Bodley & Garner, St. Augustine's School, Pendlebury, 1894–1895.

111. Frank S. Stevens School, Swansea, Massachusetts, 1908.

112. Jonathan Bourne Memorial Library, Bourne, Massachusetts, 1896–1897.

is situated. This style has the mullioned windows, and stone coped gables, and finials of Gothic, with the round arches and other characteristics of the Renaissance.[15]

While there are possible parallels between the Swansea library and Richardson's libraries of two decades earlier, an analysis of Vaughan's building would lead directly to Bodley, with a suggestion of St. Augustine's School at Pendlebury as a source (Fig. 110).

The Wren-Vaughan lantern also adorns a school that Mrs. Stevens gave to Swansea in 1908 (Fig. 111), but the work is unusual for Vaughan in that it has a full-height tetrastyle portico. The Frank S. Stevens School appears to be a reworking of the Bourne Town Library, built on Cape Cod in 1896–1897 (Fig. 112) as a memorial to Jonathan Bourne, a Cape Codder who amassed a fortune in the New Bedford whaling trade. A small one-story building with a hipped roof of red slate, the Bourne

113. Bourne Workshop for the Blind,
New York City, 1912.

Library is built of yellow brick with buff Amherst sandstone trim; instead of a portico, there is a projecting pavilion with four Tuscan pilasters. The main doorway has narrow sidelights and an elliptical fanlight, while the fenestration consists of Palladian windows set within recessed arches.

At first impression the Bourne Library, too, could be identified as an example of the Colonial Revival, but to its designer it was simply "English Renaissance of the time of Charles II."[16] Moreover, the interior, with its oak ceiling, glazed English floor tiles, and stained-glass window of St. Michael (by Clayton & Bell) hardly seems American.[17]

The Bourne Library was the first of three buildings commissioned by Emily Howland Bourne, believed to be a friend of Vaughan's. The second was the Bourne Workshop for the Blind (Fig. 113), built for the New York Association for the Blind on East 35th Street and opened October 16, 1912.[18] Used for the manufacture of mops and brooms, the Bourne Workshop had a restaurant and showers for the workers and was considered to be the most perfect industrial plant for the blind.[19]

The Bourne Workshop also represents an unusual attempt by Vaughan at commercial architecture. A five-story brick building on a standard New York lot, the facade is classically composed with three slightly recessed bays of triple windows. There is a simple cornice above the ground floor and a bracketed one between the fourth and fifth stories. The cornice brackets, quoins, and window voussoirs are the only concessions to style; otherwise, the building is straightforward, utilitarian, and dignified. As at Holy Cross Monastery, Vaughan's understated design reflects the noble and self-sacrificing deeds of the building's occupants.[20]

Vaughan's third commission for Emily Bourne was the Jonathan Bourne Whaling Museum, built in New Bedford in 1916 (Fig. 114). Located on Johnny Cake Hill (just opposite the Seamen's Bethel immortalized in Melville's *Moby Dick*), the museum was a monument to Miss Bourne's father and the industry responsible for New Bedford's brief nineteenth-century prosperity.

114. Jonathan Bourne Whaling Museum, New Bedford, Massachusetts, 1916.

131

JULY, 15 1916,

115. Bourne Whaling Museum, interior, showing construction of the Lagoda.

The museum's chief exhibit is a 60-foot, half-size replica of the bark *Lagoda,* a New Bedford whaler of the 1850s owned by Bourne. As the repository for the world's largest ship model, the museum measures 57 by 118 feet, with the weathervane atop the cupola 96 feet from the ground.[21] From the outside, the museum appears to be two stories, but the interior (Fig. 115) contains an enormous room built around the

132

116. *St. George's Ebenezer Primitive Methodist Church, Methuen, Massachusetts, 1904–1905.*

Lagoda and spanned by a barrel vault; the simple ribs spring from the columns that support side galleries. The total effect is not unlike an Early Christian basilica, or perhaps even the inside of a whale.

With the ubiquitous cupola, projecting pavilions, pilastered entrance with elliptical pediment, and Gibbsian windows, the museum is unmistakably Georgian. Although supposedly modeled on the lines of the

historic Custom House at Salem,[22] the museum's tall, somewhat elongated proportions, and the relationships of window to wall, are not
American but rather English Georgian of the age of Wren—not borrowed,
but masterfully reinterpreted by Vaughan.

Vaughan did produce one major ecclesiastical commission in the
Georgian style, St. George's Ebenezer Primitive Methodist Church in
Methuen (Fig. 116). Like All Saints Church in the same town, St. George's
was the gift of Edward Searles. Begun in 1904, St. George's is constructed
of brick, with a monumental Palladian window over the triple-arched
porch and a three-stage corner tower topped by an open belfry-cum-
cupola. Details like the Palladian window are, not surprisingly, similar
to those at the Bourne Library.

The interior of St. George's (with its basilican plan, barrel vault,
and round arches, Fig. 117) is one of Vaughan's more intriguing spatial

*117. St. George's
Church, interior.*

118. *Treat demonstration organ, photographed in 1890 in*
Old South Meeting House, Boston (now in St. George's Church, Methuen).

compositions. The entrance arches are repeated in the nave arcade, while the structural ribs defining the bays are carried right across the ceiling, foreshadowing the New Bedford Whaling Museum. The overall simplicity was purposely planned, for the focal point of the interior—and the church's *raison d'être*—is a large pipe organ which completely fills the chancel. This instrument was a demonstration organ built by the Searles-owned James Treat Company in 1889 and was in Boston's Old South Church until its removal to St. George's. The oak case, in the English Baroque manner of Grinling Gibbons (Fig. 118) was designed by Vaughan.[23]

135

119. Chime Tower at Pine Lodge, Methuen, Massachusetts, c. 1892–1895.

While Henry Vaughan's reputation is based upon his use of English Gothic, his designs in the neo-Palladian, the Georgian, and the transitional seventeenth-century styles are of considerable interest. Vaughan's preference for English Renaissance forms was as much philosophical as aesthetic—namely, English Gothic should be reserved for buildings devoted to the service of Anglo-Catholicism. But his non-Gothic works exhibit the same unmistakable Vaughan characteristics of sensibility, refinement, and a sense of wall.

One eighteenth-century-inspired design by Vaughan was neither restrained nor simple—the chime tower on Searles's Methuen estate (Fig. 119). Probably built between 1892 and 1895, this tower (now demolished) was one of the most elaborate compositions in English Renaissance ever erected in America. The tower (approximately 120 feet high) was composed of six stages, with a full array of classical details—pilasters, balustrades, entablatures, arcades, blind windows, niches, and urns, as well as a Tuscan portico at ground level. Looking like a fanciful nineteenth-century composite drawing of Wren's City churches, the chime tower carried the English Baroque of Wren and Gibbs to a conclusion only dreamed of by Colonial American church designers. Splendid as the chime tower is, it is but one of many buildings that Vaughan designed for the eccentric Edward Searles, which together form the most curious and varied chapter of Vaughan's career.[24]

6

THE PATRONAGE
OF EDWARD SEARLES

Ain't I glad that man married that woman.

Chief Justice Peters

THE CHIME tower, the Block Island summerhouse, and Searles Hall at Bowdoin are just three of the many buildings that Henry Vaughan designed for Edward Francis Searles. From the mid-1880s until his death, Vaughan was involved in dozens of Searles-sponsored projects—schools, churches, and castles; organ cases, tombs, and remodeling work. Searles was as important a patron of Vaughan as was the Episcopal Church.

While much has been written about Searles,[1] he was an even more shadowy and mysterious figure than Vaughan. In many ways, the shy and sensitive Searles must have been a lot like Vaughan, and one suspects that the client and his architect were temperamentally very compatible. Searles's life has assumed the aura of legend, and many of the stories about him seem fantastic, if not apocryphal. But it is virtually certain that Henry Vaughan designed everything that Searles built.

Edward Searles (Fig. 120) was born the son of a poor farmer in 1841 in Methuen, Massachusetts. Searles started work as a laborer in a cotton mill at the age of twelve. For about a year around 1860, he gave music lessons in Bath and Gardiner, Maine, and eventually he became a salesman for Paul & Company, "Upholsterers & Interior Decorators," in Boston. By 1875 he had joined the prestigious New York decorating firm of Herter Brothers.

Although a successful decorator, no one could have foreseen that this quiet man of such humble beginnings would become one of the wealthiest men in America. Following a trip to England in 1881—where

138

120. Edward F. Searles and his mother at Pine Lodge, c. 1894.

he may have met Vaughan and perhaps encouraged him to emigrate to this country—Searles resigned from Herter Brothers for reasons of ill health and took a trip to California in 1883. In San Francisco Searles visited the widow of the Southern Pacific Railroad magnate Mark Hopkins, for whom Herter Brothers had decorated a mansion on Nob Hill. Mrs. Hopkins (who was twenty-one years Searles's senior) fell in love with the 42-year-old Searles and proposed marriage.

Searles and Mrs. Hopkins did not marry until 1887, when she gave him the building at No. 1 Broadway in New York and controlling interest in *The Globe,* a New York newspaper, as wedding presents, but he did supervise the construction, as well as the decoration, certain improvements, and the building of some additions of Mrs. Hopkins's estate in

Great Barrington, Massachusetts, from about 1884 until its completion in 1888.

Kellogg Terrace (also known as "Barrington House" and the "Searles Mansion") is a late-medieval/early-Renaissance French-style granite mansion designed in 1885 by McKim, Mead & White. Searles made a number of changes to the house and the estate, including the interior decoration and the construction of a new entrance gateway (designed by Vaughan). Predating the main house was a stone carriage house and a coachman's quarters, both of which burned in 1885. Although it is not known if Vaughan originally designed these two structures, he certainly was responsible for the rebuilding of the carriage house, called the Marigold, a project completed in 1897 (Fig. 121).[2] Vaughan surely must have decorated the English Baroque music room at Kellogg Terrace, for he designed the 25-foot oak case for the giant pipe organ that Searles installed

121. Kellogg Terrace, Great Barrington, Massachusetts, carriage house and coachman's quarters, c. 1882.

122. Kellogg Terrace, Music Room, c. 1885–1886.

there (Fig. 122) —the first of several notable organ cases that Vaughan created for Searles.[3] Also, Vaughan almost certainly designed the Windsor Room at Kellogg Terrace, built to house a set of doors allegedly brought from Windsor Castle and later moved to Stanton Harcourt, the Searles Castle in Windham, New Hampshire. The intricate, Tudor-style plaster ceiling remains.

Although the house on Block Island was completed shortly after Searles's marriage, the newlyweds devoted much of their energy to

141

completely remodeling Pine Lodge, the house in Methuen where Searles
was born. And it was there that Mrs. Searles died in 1891.

Mrs. Searles left her entire estate to her husband—a quarter share
in the Southern Pacific Railroad and property valued at at least $21
million. Her adopted son Timothy Hopkins contested the will, and, in a
highly publicized trial, Thomas Hubbard successfully defended Searles's
inheritance. After the trial, General Hubbard suggested that Searles donate
a science building to Bowdoin College in Mrs. Searles's memory.[4] Another
Vaughan-designed memorial to Mrs. Searles was the case for the Treat
organ in Grace Church, San Francisco.[5]

Searles's financially advantageous marital union had allowed him to
indulge a whim for building and he undertook major changes to the
simple Federal-period farmhouse in Methuen and the estate he was amassing around it. Eventually Pine Lodge consisted of several hundred acres
surrounded by castle walls, behind which stood the greatly expanded
house, two chime towers, and a variety of half-timbered buildings and
workers' cottages.[6]

123. Pine Lodge, Methuen, c. 1887–1915 (photograph taken c. 1890).

*124. Pine Lodge,
the organ from the
Broadway Tabernacle.*

While the main house has since been greatly altered, Searles continually added to it during the remainder of his life. Old photographs (Fig. 123) show that it had a complex, picturesque skyline, a colonnade surrounding the house, and at least two large cupolas. The complex configuration of the otherwise plain frame house was unified by the Ionic columns of the colonnade, pilasters, and a seemingly endless array of balustrades. The interior decoration—to complement Searles's collection of art treasures consisting of tapestries, sculpture, and jewelry, as well as painting—was certainly done by him, but the exterior details were clearly in Vaughan's English Palladian style.

143

125. Pine Lodge, chapel (completed 1918) and the stone bell tower, 1896.

Perhaps the most unusual feature of the seventy-four-room house was the narrow, three-story vestibule between the entry hall and the great hall known as the "Marble Museum." About 15 feet wide, this dramatic groin-vaulted Baroque space contained an 1859 three-manual Ferris & Stuart organ brought from the Broadway Tabernacle in New York. The new case, with angels playing flutes and trumpets and featuring a bust of Johann Sebastian Bach, was undoubtedly by Vaughan (Fig. 124). The organ was the focus of concerts and lavish parties; for a Christmas Eve gathering in 1890, organ-builder James Treat was Santa Claus.

Of the several half-timbered buildings and cottages on the estate, the gate lodge (built in 1900) is the most interesting. Here the half-timbering (above a ground floor of ashlar granite) has infill not of stucco but of herringbone-patterned brick. Also unusual is the elaborate floral carving around the oriel window and on the bargeboard. The whole effect is a rather academic expression of Tudor Gothic, for example, more like the work of Cope & Stewardson of this period than the simpler half-timbering of Vaughan's earlier career.

But the most impressive—and most typically Vaughan—building on the Methuen property is the stone chapel visible beyond the battlemented walls of the estate (Fig. 125). Reputed to have cost $600,000,

126. Searles High School, Methuen, Massachusetts, 1904–1905.

the narrow chapel (with a burial crypt underneath) is composed of three bays with a square, three-stage buttressed tower.[7] Except for the Decorated windows, this mausoleum is almost devoid of exterior ornament.[8]

Apart from occasional parties for friends, Searles lived like a recluse behind his fortresslike walls. He did, however, cancel the town's debt of $65,000 in 1900, gave the town thousands of trees, and procured for Methuen a monumental statue of Washington by Thomas Ball. He was rarely seen, and then only when he drove out in his gold-trimmed Pierce-Arrow to supervise one of the many buildings he donated to his home town.

These many gifts included three churches (All Saints, St. George's, and Emmanuel Primitive Methodist Church—a simple half-timber structure built in 1901), the railroad station, a battlemented bridge across the Spiket River, the Red Tavern (a 1900 half-timbered recreation of an English inn), a boardinghouse called the Hayloft, and the John Hancock Masonic Lodge (both earlier buildings that were remodeled, the latter with Inigo Jones-like classical details,) the Central Grammar School, Searles High School, two family tombs, an organ factory, and an organ recital hall. Of these, the high school and the organ hall are the most significant.

145

Designed in about 1904 or 1905, the Searles High School (Fig. 126) was built with an endowment fund of $1 million and required the services of imported Italian workmen.[9] One of Vaughan's largest academic buildings, the limestone-trimmed brick school is a variation on the Jacobean style that emerged at Searles and Hubbard halls at Bowdoin a few years earlier. In fact, Searles High School is a recreation of an English prodigy house. Three monumental stories in height, Searles High School is a long block with three projecting pavilions (connected by open loggias or arcades), complete with a full-height oriel window in the central pavilion. While not as picturesque as Hubbard Hall, the Methuen high school is a noble exercise in the Jacobean style as applied to American institutional architecture.

In 1889 Searles bought an 1840s textile mill which Vaughan remodeled into an organ factory for James E. Treat. Treat was a native of New Haven who probably met Searles while he was employed by Hutchings, Plaisted & Company in Boston (Searles purchased a Hutchings organ in

127. Serlo Organ Hall, Methuen, Massachusetts, 1899–1909.

146

128. Serlo Organ Hall, interior.

1880). The factory contained a two-story test hall, which, with its column-supported gallery, heavy tabernacle Palladian doorways and window frames, and massive ceiling beams, looks remarkably like the great hall in Inigo Jones's Queen's House in Greenwich (1616–1635).[10]

The Serlo Organ Hall, which Vaughan began in 1899, was dedicated in 1909. The instrument for which the organ hall was constructed was originally built in 1857–1863 in Ludwigsburg, Germany by E. F. Walcker & Company for the Boston Music Hall.[11] In 1897, after the Music Hall was demolished, Searles bought the organ for $1,500. The exterior of the brick organ hall (Fig. 127) is extremely simple, with very high and narrow proportions; despite a tall Italianate campanile and an elaborate gable with Baroque volutes, it is a variant of Vaughan's Anglo-Dutch style. This rather unassuming exterior gives little clue to the building's incredibly rich Baroque interior (Fig. 128). While the organ case is German Baroque in style, designed by Gustave Herter before his emigration to New York, the stylistic details and spatial arrangement of the interior are pure Wren (for example, St. Stephen, Walbrook, 1662–1687). The undulating organ case with its lower level supported by caryatids, and featuring putti and a bust of Bach, sits in the building's domed crossing which was designed not for large audiences, but for private concerts. In its exuberance and scholarly re-creation of English Baroque details, Serlo Organ Hall ranks with the chapel at St. Paul's School as one of Vaughan's most complete historicist compositions—and one of his most dramatic.

In the 1890s Searles, whose passion for building equaled his desire for seclusion, began buying extensive tracts of farmland over the border in the town of Salem, New Hampshire. On his 1,600 acres in Salem, Searles proceeded to create a self-contained rural community that would supply Pine Lodge with dairy products, as well as ice and spring water. Like the Methuen estate, the Searles farm, known as Dairy Court, or more popularly as Stillwater Manor, was surrounded with high walls, behind which the unabashed Anglophile ruled like a medieval baron. The main house is a picturesque brick, masonry, and half-timber evocation of a Tudor country estate (Fig. 129). One of the several cottages that Vaughan designed for the Salem farm was described as if it was "a medieval serf's dwelling transplanted, foundation and all, from the old world."[12]

129. Stillwater Manor, Salem, New Hampshire, 1898–1905.

130. Searles School, Windham, New Hampshire, 1907–1908.

About the time Searles began work on Stillwater he presented Salem with a gift of the renovation of the Salem Town Hall, or Old Meeting House, built in 1738. Vaughan's restoration was not well received, for, although the structure had been modified for civic use in 1846, Searles had the ceiling torn out and new beams installed.[13] If residents were less than pleased with the work at the Old Meeting House, Searles did at least donate a new church to Salem Methodists after their church was destroyed by fire in 1909. The half-timbered North Salem United Methodist Church was begun in 1910 and completed the following year.

When Searles's attempts to buy some neighboring farmland were thwarted by a local farmer who refused to sell, Searles bought a 1,400-acre tract of land in the neighboring town of Windham and constructed his last major project, a stone castle known as Stanton Harcourt.

Even though the new estate was also surrounded by high stone fortifications, Searles felt that the village school was too close and offered to build Windham a new schoolhouse if the town would give him the existing structure. The offer was accepted in November 1906, and the new schoolhouse, considered the "handsomest and finest small school building in the state," was completed in early 1909.[14]

Since the Searles School in Windham (Fig. 130) was designed to serve as both schoolhouse and chapel, the plan is accordingly two wings

131. Stanton Harcourt, Windham, New Hampshire, c. 1907–1915.

in the form of an L joined by a crenelated chime tower. The tower, and walls up to sill level, are of local granite, but the upper walls are half-timbered; the roof is slate with copper flashing, while cypress and beech are used inside. A more modest structure than Searles High School in Methuen (Searles said the building cost over $40,000), the Windham structure is an especially attractive, if unusual, New England village schoolhouse.[15]

The castle across the road from the schoolhouse is also Tudor Gothic in style. A genealogical search had linked Searles with the Oxfordshire Harcourts, whose fifteenth-century manor house, Stanton Harcourt, had

150

largely been pulled down in 1780, leaving only a Tudor gatehouse, a kitchen, and a tower, known as "Pope's Tower".[16] Searles is said to have sent Vaughan to England to reconstruct on paper the destroyed section of the original Stanton Harcourt, "after which he built this castle in Windham."[17]

Constructed of granite with red sandstone trim, Stanton Harcourt is situated on a hilltop with a commanding view of Canobie Lake and the surrounding hills (Fig. 131). The castle is L-shaped in plan and forms a large courtyard. Approached by a portcullis with working machinery (designed to discourage intruders, provided they got past the eight-foot

151

outer walls), the castle's wings spread between two large battlemented blocks, each with various ancillary turrets and observation towers. The steep, sloping exterior walls give the castle a foreboding and convincingly medieval appearance, although the courtyard facade is not unlike the baronial castles built by the Victorians in the Highlands of Scotland.

Whether or not Europe's finest masons and woodworkers were imported to work on the interior decorations (as local tradition holds), the castle's furnishings and fittings make the reputed cost of $1,250,000 believable. [18] The main salon contains a marble fireplace that was formerly in the Tuileries in Paris (and for which Searles paid $50,000), while other fireplaces are of Italian marble. The floors are laid with marble and with tiles from the Moravian Tile Works of the American Arts and Crafts potter Henry Mercer. [19] Vaughan's ability to design wood carving (as seen in the churches, as well as in the organ cases) is further demonstrated at Stanton Harcourt by the oak-paneled walls with their delicate linen folds, by the timbered ceilings, and in the many smaller decorations like the Searles escutcheons on the walls.

Stanton Harcourt was begun sometime after 1905, and its construction and furnishing took the better part of a decade. The castle, now a secretarial school and religious retreat, is still an impressive composition. While not one of Vaughan's best designs—its size alone must have made it something of a chore—Stanton Harcourt is more than just a curiosity. It is another instance of Vaughan's introduction into America of one of the many phases of English medieval architecture.

Since both Vaughan and Searles were such enigmatic characters and as neither left any writing about their collaboration, it is perhaps pointless to speculate on their relationship. In fact, it is hard to gauge exactly what Searles's patronage meant to Vaughan's career. Searles's continual financial support in the form of endless commissions from the mid-1880s onward may have allowed the English émigré a certain measure of security, especially for an architect who actively refused to seek work. However, Searles's constant building projects may have drained Vaughan's creative energies, for surely there cannot have been much challenge in designing stone walls and remodeling older structures.

But the personal aspects of the Vaughan-Searles partnership aside, the fact remains that Searles was responsible for such Vaughan masterworks as the Searles Science Building at Bowdoin, All Saints Church, Methuen, and that splendid example of Wren-Gibbsian Baroque, the Serlo Organ Hall.

7

THE ARCHITECTURE OF HENRY VAUGHAN: STYLE AND SYMBOL

The little bare office in Boston was typical of his unworldliness. It seemed a shrine, in which no earthly or sordid thoughts could dwell. And the man who stood behind the tall desk was like a saint out of a picture . . . . He had no artistic conceit to immortalize his own ideas: with such dreams as God gave him, he fused the dreams of those who pleaded for his help, and the unity which resulted was evidence of a generous willingness to listen as well as to teach.

Charles Lewis Slattery, *Certain American Faces*, 1918

IF THERE is one word that would most appropriately describe Vaughan, it would be "pious." For Vaughan, architecture and religion were inseparable. Vaughan attended mass every day at St. John the Evangelist, the dour and somewhat forbidding American bastion of the Cowley Fathers situated between his office on Pemberton Square and his rooming house on Beacon Hill. He was, above all, a "Christian and a churchman of the truest and best type, devoid of cant and hypocrisy," a man "who walked humbly with his God and delighted in doing good."[1]

Vaughan was, as we have seen, a reserved and solitary man, something less than a romantic figure. As Charles Lewis Slattery, William Lawrence's successor as Bishop of Massachusetts, recalled: "Few people ever saw Henry Vaughan. I cannot remember hearing that he ever made a speech or appeared on any public platform."[2] It would be impossible to imagine Vaughan as a suitable subject for the historical novelist. After describing the architect's quiet and self-effacing personality (and perhaps conjecturing upon Vaughan's relationship with Elizabeth Stevens or Mary Bradford Foote, see Fig. 137), such an author would be left with only the buildings as a key to his subject's spirit. Although he revealed little of his private life, Henry Vaughan was "a great silent force . . . a man who said nothing, but did much."[3]

153

Even when using buildings as the focus of Vaughan's influence, the historian is beset with many problems. Not the least of these is the fact that Vaughan's career follows no logical pattern of development. Instead of recognizable growth or change (say, from his earlier to his later works), a building such as the chapel at St. Paul's School (Fig. 133) is just as mature and as accomplished as the Church of the Redeemer of almost thirty years later. He did, however, tend to design in groups. The small parish churches were usually built in half-timber, the larger churches in masonry, and the school buildings in brick, and the works in these groups were often variations of a dominant theme. For example, the similarities of St. Barnabas, St. Thomas's, and St. Martin's suggest that Vaughan was momentarily preoccupied with a single conception of the stone village church.

There is also little reason to suspect that Vaughan would have appreciably changed his style or his total decorative approach had he remained in Britain. Similarly, his being in this country hardly affected or modified his work (there is almost no direct influence from Richardson, for example). Yet Vaughan's presence in America—even if seen only in a limited sense as an extension of George Frederick Bodley to these shores—did serve as an inspiration to a certain group of younger American architects, and his churches were models for a renewed Gothic revival. Vaughan's re-creation of the Gothic Middle Ages offered a tangible illustration of the possibilities of glorious Catholic religious expression: Vaughan not only persuaded Cram and other architects that their architectural salvation lay in English Gothic, but he prevented their conversion to Rome. The Counter Reformation was the last time Roman Catholicism had contributed to ecclesiastical art in a meaningful way, and there was no architectural revival in the Roman camp as powerful and as appealing as Bodley and Vaughan's pre-Reformation-inspired Gothicism.[4]

A comparison of Vaughan's early works (such as St. Paul's or some of the parish churches) with some of the monuments of the Victorian Gothic style demonstrates the changes effected by Vaughan's assured and historically correct Bodlean Gothic. Churches such as Cummings & Sears' New Old South Church (1874) on Boston's Copley Square (Fig. 4), R. M. Upjohn's nearby Central Congregational Church of 1866 (Fig. 132), or even the Old Chapel at St. Paul's (Fig. 133), relied on a variety of medieval sources, as well as on the interpretation of Venetian Gothic that was popularized by John Ruskin. From the standpoint of architectural design, it doesn't really matter that the genealogy of the Victorian Gothicists' work is sometimes hard to trace, for the results are undeniably

132. R. M. Upjohn, Central Congregational Church, Boston, 1866.

133. St. Paul's School, old and new chapels.

impressive. However, the massing and the skylines of their compositions are rather complicated when compared to Vaughan's churches. St. Paul's and Groton are far simpler, their outlines are unified and compact, the broad, unadorned expanses of roof complement the canonical sense of wall—and they are clearly and firmly rooted in the English Middle Ages.

While Vaughan avoided the so-called Ruskinian styles, aesthetically he remained very much a Victorian. Even in his most historicist compositions, Vaughan's reliance upon and patronage of such English Arts and Crafts designers as C. E. Kempe, John Evans, and Robert Casson, and the resultant decorative richness are quite different from the sometimes arid compositions of his Modern Gothic followers. It is difficult to imagine that a collegiate chapel such as Cram's chapel at St. George's School of 1924 (Fig. 134) could have been designed without knowledge of Vaughan's pioneering work at St. Paul's and Groton. Like St. George's, the chapel at Trinity College, Hartford, by Vaughan's Washington successors Frohman, Robb & Little (1932, Fig. 135) lacks the warmth and color that characterized Vaughan's best work; it is correct, but somehow mechanical, even cold.

However, there is little if any indication of an individual interpretation of Gothic in Vaughan's architecture, such as that which marked

156

134. Ralph Adams Cram, St. George's School Chapel, Newport, Rhode Island, 1924.

135. Frohman, Robb & Little, Trinity College Chapel, Hartford, Connecticut, 1932.

157

136. Montacute House, Montacute, Somerset, c. 1599.

the work of Modern Gothicists like Bertram Goodhue or Charles Klauder—designers who combined eclecticism and twentieth-century modernism. And certainly, Vaughan showed no interest in the new architectural developments of his time, or in employing anything other than time-honored building techniques. Although we know too little of the actual mechanics of his constructions, Vaughan's buildings offer almost nothing unusual in terms of structure.

Vaughan was intensely preoccupied with details, yet the total effect of his architecture transcends its impeccable historicism—whether Gothic or Georgian. He did indeed borrow freely from his English mentors, particularly Bodley, as he did from the Middle Ages. Also, few architects in America used English neo-Palladian sources so extensively. The sources are always English, whether from Bodley & Garner, Inigo Jones, or Wren. Searles Hall at Bowdoin and the Methuen High School, for example, clearly owe much to Garner's Hewell Grange, which itself is indebted to Montacute House (Fig. 136). Yet Montacute is as acceptable a model for an American building as the French chateaux that provided the vocabulary for Richard Morris Hunt or the Renaissance palaces that inspired Charles McKim. And, though hitherto unappreciated, the results that

158

Vaughan achieved are no less stunning or no less significant than the work of these creative eclectics.

It has been fashionable to denigrate the works of Vaughan and his contemporaries because they sought inspiration in the Middle Ages and because they failed to live up to some preconceived notion of expanding the boundaries of modern architecture. Fortunately, the recent reassessment of men of Vaughan's generation and the High Victorians that preceded them—to say nothing of the current revision of modernism itself—allows a new understanding of the value of their considerable architectural achievement.

Perhaps there are still those who might see Vaughan's architecture as a faintly ludicrous manifestation of an American cultural inferiority complex—a striving for English roots, the trappings of respectability. Rather, it should be interpreted as an earnest reminder of age-old religious traditions and artistic principles.

137. Gravestone of Mary Bradford Foote,
Mt. Auburn Cemetery, Cambridge, Massachusetts, 1912.

Groton, St. Paul's, and the many parish churches represent the finest flowering of the Gothic Revival in America. Vaughan's buildings are the best argument for his placement in the pantheon of notable American scholar-architects, along with Upjohn, McKim, and Cram. But because of Vaughan's modesty and shyness, his absolute refusal to proselytize, he has been overlooked. The late nineteenth century was a glorious age, particularly in New England, and in architecture not a little of this glory was the work of Henry Vaughan.

138. St. Paul's School Chapel, consecration stone.

NOTES

INTRODUCTION

1. John Coolidge, "Gothic Revival Churches in New England and New York," unpublished thesis, Harvard College, 1935, 229.

2. Edward B. Gammons, organist of Groton School, tells a story about Frank Cleveland, a partner in the firm of Cram, Goodhue & Ferguson, who fell asleep while riding on the train from Worcester to Nashua. Just as the train was passing near the school, the English-born Cleveland suddenly awoke and, seeing the tower of the chapel, thought for a moment that he was back in his native Somerset (interview, August 15, 1969).

3. Henry Vaughan "revitalized the Gothic style as McKim, Mead & White had reinstituted classicism." L. M. Roth, *A Concise History of American Architecture,* New York, 1979, 253. In the chapter on "The Development of Ecclesiastical Architecture in America" in his book *The Gothic Quest* (New York, 1907, 139–164), Cram, in effect, asked the rhetorical question "After Richardson, what next?" Cram's answer was, of course, Vaughan.

4. In his *American Architecture Since 1780,* Cambridge, Mass., 1969, Marcus Whiffen cites Cram's All Saints' Church in Ashmont, Mass. (1891) as the seminal work of the Late Gothic Revival (p. 173). However, Cram used the term in an article on "Good and Bad Modern Gothic," *(Architectural Review,* VI, August, 1899, 115–119), in which Vaughan's St. Paul's School Chapel is discussed. Obviously, Cram does not mean "modern" in the sense of the modern movement of the International Style, etc., but rather a new, or contemporary, Gothic based primarily on the English Perpendicular style.

5. David B. Emerson, "Henry Vaughan," *Architectural Record,* 42, September, 1917, 286.

6. Henry F. Withey and Elise R. Withey, *Biographical Dictionary of American Architects (Deceased),* Los Angeles, 1956, 618.

7. Ralph Adams Cram, *My Life in Architecture,* Boston, 1936, 39.

8. For a complete discussion of the ecclesiological movement in America see P. B. Stanton, *The Gothic Revival and American Church Architecture,* Baltimore, 1968; the English background is discussed in J. F. White, *The Cambridge Movement,* Cambridge, 1962.

9. Ralph Adams Cram, *Church Building,* Boston, 1914, 264.

10. David B. Emerson, "A thing of beauty is a joy forever," *The Harvester,* 17, September 11, 1917, 1. Vaughan's important position in the revival of Gothic was well recognized in his own day. For example, the *Architectural Review,* VII, June 1899, 88, wrote: "A few of our architects familiar with Gothic ideas and principles, notably Messrs. Cram, Goodhue & Ferguson, Vaughan, Cope & Stewardson, and some others have recently made very successful use of English Gothic in church work. Then also come the imitators, who know nothing of Gothic, imagine that a few pointed arches, however poorly shaped, a few pinnacles, however awkward and unreasonable, and some traceried windows, generally of wood and most inharmonious design make Gothic architecture. In their souls really condemning Gothic, they vainly imagine that anybody can do a Gothic Church."

11. Letter from Marjorie Raphael, Mother Superior, Sisters of St. Margaret, Boston, October 26, 1969. Vaughan apparently came to America "especially for the building of St. Margaret's Chapel, representing Mr. Bodley" (*St. Margaret's Quarterly,* January 1922, 6).

12. Episcopal female religious orders were a definite outgrowth of the English High Church movement; the Sisters of St. Margaret were founded by John Mason Neale in 1855.

13. If Vaughan wished to set up his own practice, Bodley, as his mentor and employer, may have advised him to go to America. More likely, Vaughan came to America as Bodley's emissary and decided to stay. Personal reasons, such as a spurned marriage proposal, cannot be ruled out.

14. Vaughan, a fellow of the American Institute of Architects and the Boston Society of Architects, was awarded a silver medal for architecture at the Louisiana Purchase Exposition in St. Louis in 1904, as well as honorary degrees from Bowdoin (1894) and Yale (1907). Referring to the Yale degree, Vaughan wrote the Bishop of Washington, "I don't know how it came about" (Vaughan to Henry Yates Satterlee, July 20, 1907, Washington Cathedral Archives).

15. A major exhibition on Cram was held at the Boston Public Library and in New York in 1975. The show was organized and the catalogue written by Douglass Shand Tucci; see Tucci's *Ralph Adams Cram: American Medievalist,* Boston, 1975 and *Church Building in Boston 1720–1970,* Boston, 1974.

16. Paul Goldberger, "Architects Meet to Note Failures of Modernism," *New York Times,* December 11, 1981, C19.

17. George E. Barton, "Henry Vaughan," *Journal of the American Institute of Architects,* 5, 1917, 518.

18. Clarence H. Blackall, "Henry Vaughan," *American Architect,* CXII, July 11, 1917, 31.

19. Upon Vaughan's death, Dean G. C. F. Bratenahl of Washington Cathedral wrote to Vaughan's executor, Robert Casson: "I earnestly trust that you will be able to secure for the Cathedral all of Mr. Vaughan's drawings and papers relating to Church architecture." (letter, July 13, 1917, Washington Cathedral Archives). Although later correspondence in the Bodley & Vaughan file imply that such drawings were obtained for the Cathedral, their present whereabouts is unknown.

CHAPTER 1

1. Letter from Rosemary Vaughan (granddaughter of Henry Vaughan's brother William), Colyton, Devon, June 21, 1970. Although never listed in the General Register Office, Vaughan's birth is recorded in the family bible. Vaughan was related to the seventeenth-century Metaphysical poet of the same name, as well as to the composer Ralph Vaughan Williams.

2. Interview with A. Ronald Vaughan (Vaughan's nephew and godson), Seaton, Devon, October 9, 1970. Unfortunately, Dollar Academy's records were lost in a fire in the 1950s. A book awarded to Vaughan as a second prize in English survives; the medal is inscribed: "Henry Vaughan, Glasgow Stages 2B, 22C." Of Vaughan's two sisters, Elizabeth (born 1839) is believed to have administered the fatal dose of lead lotion to her father, as she later declared herself to be the Virgin Mary and used to ride about in an open carriage bestowing benedictions (Rosemary Vaughan, June 21, 1970). Emma Frances (born 1838) followed Henry to Boston, apparently causing him some embarrass-ment: "I am very sorry I could not come when you first asked me. I had to meet my sister who had come from England to attend the Temperance Convention" (Vaughan to Bishop Satterlee, October 18, 1906, Washington Cathedral).

3. Rosemary Vaughan, ibid. The RIBA did not operate an architectural school and Vaughan is not listed in the records of the Architectural Association for the period 1860–1873.

4. Letter from Yvonne Vaughan, Colyton, Devon, January 6, 1970. William was Henry's closest sibling, being eighteen months his senior. It is interesting to note that William was "a complete extrovert," and his son said that he was "always booming," while he remembered his uncle Henry as "a very diffident man with a pleasant quiet voice."

5. Henry Vaughan, "The Late George Frederick Bodley," *Architectural Review*, 14, 1907, 213; Vaughan to Satterlee, October 22, 1907.

6. "George Frederick Bodley," *Architect & Contract Reporter*, 78, October 25, 1970, 258.

7. Edward Warren, "George Frederick Bodley, R. A.," *Architectural Review*, 11, 1902, 30.

8. Emerson, "Henry Vaughan," p. 286; "Buried in a Vault Under P. E. Chapel," *Evening Star* (Washington), November 2, 1917.

9. Thomas Garner (1839–1906), also a pupil of Scott's, joined Bodley in partnership in 1869. Although they collaborated on some projects, "for the most part they divided the work, Mr. Bodley taking first one building, then Mr. Garner another" (Vaughan, "Bodley," 213). The partnership was dissolved in 1897 when Garner became a Roman Catholic. Bodley then enlisted the help of Cecil Greenwood Hare; Bodley left his architectural drawings to Hare.

10. St. Michael's was greatly enlarged by William Burges, and by J. S. Chapple after Burges's death. See John Betjeman, ed., *An American's Guide to English Parish Churches*, New York, 1958, 367. "Bodley, after a brilliant beginning in the High Victorian style, turned his back on it as early as the mid-1860s, initiating the predominant mode of the Late Victorian period" (Roger Dixon and Stefan Methesius, *Victorian Architecture*, London, 1978, 203–204).

11. Vaughan, "Bodley," p. 213. In fact, Bodley believed that his upholding of English Gothic was responsible for his being recognized by the Royal Institute of British Architects with their highest award: "I think I owe this honour to receiving the gold medal more especially to my great love for that style of architecture which I have always held, and do hold, to be the most beautiful style—I mean the English Gothic of the Middle Ages" ("Bodley," *Architect & Contract*, 258).

12. David Verey, "G. F. Bodley," in Jane Fawcett, ed., *Seven Victorian Architects*, London, 1976, 95.

13. Vaughan, "Bodley," 213. *Victorian Church Art*, the catalogue of the exhibition held at the Victoria and Albert Museum in the winter of 1971–1972, has a section devoted to "G. F. Bodley and his circle" (pp. 111–119); among the Bodley works exhibited were textiles, communion services, a crucifix, a font cover, a brass rubbing, a crozier, a cope, and two gilded angels.

14. In speaking of the influence of the teachings of Pugin, D. D. Sedding told the Arts Congress in Liverpool in 1888: "We should have had no Morris, no Street, no Burges, no Shaw, no Webb, no Bodley, no Rossetti, no Burne-Jones, no Crane, but for Pugin" (Lionel Lambourne, *Utopian Craftsmen*, Salt Lake City, 1980, 9); it is interesting to note that Bodley is accorded equal status with his better-remembered contemporaries. Given Bodley's patronage of Morris et al., Vaughan undoubtedly must have known these men too. Bodley was also a close friend of William Butterfield's, while Street was a fellow pupil of Scott's.

15. According to Edward Warren, it was Bodley who gave Morris "the opportunity of his first essay in church glass" ("The Works of Messrs. Bodley and Garner," *Architectural Review*, VI, 1899, 26). Kempe, one of the most important Victorian stained-glass makers—along with Morris and Selwyn Image, was also trained and "started on his successful career by Bodley" (Vaughan, "Bodley," 213). The literature on Kempe (1837–1907) is extremely sparse. The 1980 U.S. Christmas stamp depicted a Kempe window in Vaughan's Bethlehem Chapel at Washington Cathedral, actually done by Kempe's art director, John William Lisle. "Vaughan was the American representative for all Kempe glass made for this country. It was ordered from England, the glass came in a boat to its destination in this country with Mr. Vaughan handling the final steps" (Louise B. Richardson to Rev. David Boulton, Christ Church, New Haven, October 9, 1980). Margaret Stavridi, daughter of John William Lisle, and James Weatherley are preparing a book on Kempe. A settle designed by Bodley and Kempe is at Wightwick Manor, the Morris-decorated house near Wolverhampton.

16. "Our work is so confused, so mystified by many styles. In old days there was a unity of feeling . . . . And now we think so much of our styles and do not think enough of what we have to express, what we have to say, what we have to tell the world" (Bodley, *Architect & Contract*, 258). The Scottish architect Charles Rennie Mackintosh, in a lecture to the Glasgow Institute of Architects in 1893, singled out Belcher, Shaw, Sedding, Stokes, Bentley, and Bodley as those men whom he felt were doing "designs by living men for living men" (Alistair Service, *Edwardian Architecture*, London, 1977, 44).

17. Warren, "Bodley and Garner," 27–28. Bodley, Garner, and G. G. Scott, Jr.,

founded their own firm, Watts & Co., in Hampstead to produce church furnishings to their own designs (Verey, "Bodley," 96).

18. In his patronage of Kempe, as well as the English glass firm of Clayton & Bell and the American glazier Charles Connick, along with the Oberammergau-trained wood-carver Johannes Kirchmayer, the Welsh stone-carver John Evans, and the wood-working firm of Irving & Casson, Vaughan supported a group of artisans which could be called an American Arts and Crafts school.

19. Vaughan, "Bodley," 213. It has been said that Vaughan was noted for his reviews of Gothic architecture, but this is the only article by Vaughan located to date. However, "the Parish Club were given an instructive lecture at their March meeting on the growth of ecclesiastical architecture as illustrated in the Cathedrals of England. The lecturer was Mr. Henry Vaughan, the well–known architect" ("Church Notes," Church of the Advent, Boston, II, April, 1892, 49).

20. "Bodley," *Architect & Contract*, 258. "Shy, reserved, and sensitive, he shrank from publicity, and always avoided, as far as he could, speeches, lectures, or official functions" (Edward Warren, "The Late G. F. Bodley, R.A.," *Architectural Review*, XXIII, November 1907, 231). As Vaughan reported, Bodley did most of his designing "in the quiet of his country home, going to the office only when obliged to do so" (Vaughan, "Bodley," 213); this would suggest an even greater role than usual for his head draftsman.

21. Vaughan, "Bodley," 213.

22. Halsey Wood, Jr. to R. Craig Miller, April 26, 1970. The Wood-Vaughan association was brought to my attention by Dr. Miller, who wrote a master's thesis on Wood for the University of Delaware. Family legend claims that "a visiting American, who wanted to set up a memorial to his recently departed wife" was going to take Vaughan "to all the European capitals and that Henry would then draw up plans for the memorial" (R. Vaughan, June 21, 1970. This most likely is a garbled memory of Vaughan's association with Edward F. Searles; see Chapter 6).

23. Wood's widow, Florence Hemsley Wood, stated that Wood knew various leading architects like Carrère, Hastings, McKim, and Vaughan (*Memories of William Halsey Wood*, Philadelphia, 1938, 40). One of Vaughan's early works, the Church of St. John Evangelist, Tannersville, N.Y. (1884), was built by Florence Hemsley's family.

24. Cram, *My Life*, 36.

25. C. N. Field, "The Society of St. Margaret," *Church Militant*, XII, February 1909, 8.

26. "For years he was to be found only in his office, in the Church of St. John the Evangelist, or at a certain restaurant where he took his solitary meals" (Cram, "Masters in Architecture—Langford Warren, Henry Vaughan," *Boston Transcript*, July 2, 1917). In 1906 Vaughan designed a rood screen for St. John's. The most complete discussion of High Church Anglicanism in Boston is found in Douglass Shand Tucci, *Church Building in Boston, 1720–1970* (Boston: 1974), see also Ralph Adams Cram, *My Life in Architecture*, Boston: 1936.

27. Norman Joseph Catir, Jr., *Saint Stephen's Church in Providence*, Providence, 1964, 61. In 1893 Vaughan designed the wrought-iron gates for the rood screen (p. 77). The

work at St. Stephen's cost $4,000—as much as the entire St. Andrew's Church in Newcastle, Maine, of the same year (*American Architect and Building News*, 14, August 18, 1883, 399).

28. George Wolfe Shinn, *King's Handbook of Notable Episcopal Churches in the United States*, Boston, 1889, 103.

29. Barton, "Vaughan," 518. Barton mentions how he once approached Vaughan with "advance information concerning a new church building," and how "influential friends" could ensure Vaughan the commission. Vaughan replied: "Certainly not. If my work is good and they want it, it will come to me." Pemberton Square, now demolished, was a small enclave of three- and four-story brick houses where many Boston architects had their offices. Vaughan lived in rooms at No. 10 and, from 1886 to 1916, No. 80 Pickney Street, and after that at 2 Mt. Vernon Street.

30. Interview with Lloyd Hendrick, conducted by Richard T. Feller, Clerk of the Works, Washington Cathedral, at Bourne, Massachusetts, July 20, 1967 (tape, Washington Cathedral Archives).

31. Henry Vaughn [sic], Certificate of Death, City of Newton, Mass., July 5, 1917. Although Vaughan's place of burial is listed as Forest Hills, he was interred in Washington Cathedral on November 1, 1917. Vaughan's brother William attended the Washington burial.

32. Rosemary Vaughan, June 21, 1970. Miss Vaughan believed that the family Vaughan lived with was the Frank S. Stevenses, although they lived in Swansea, Massachusetts. Mr. Stevens died in 1898, but in 1927 Mrs. Stevens gave $75,000 to Washington Cathedral for one of the great crossing piers, in Vaughan's memory. Vaughan designed three buildings in Swansea for Mrs. Stevens, as well as the bronze doors on Mr. Stevens's tomb. "The relationship between Vaughan and Elizabeth Stevens is still a matter of conjecture. However, Elizabeth was a lady who held great attraction for men and it has been said that Vaughan was one of her ardent admirers, and lived at the Stevens home much of the period when the building of the Church and Library was in progress" (Rev. Allen W. Joslin, February 22, 1981). Vaughan's rooming house on Mt. Vernon Street was demolished to make way for a new addition to the Massachusetts State House and this may explain his residency at Casson's.

33. Emerson, "Vaughan," 286.

34. Blackall, "Vaughan," *American Architect*, 31.

CHAPTER 2

1. Vaughan also designed a house in Newcastle for the Gliddens about this time (see Chapter 5). Vaughan came to America on William Glidden's packet boat *Atlantic Clipper* (where they presumably met) and Vaughan lived with the Gliddens while building the church and house. Susanna Coggeshall, in her article "A Brief History of St. Andrew's Parish in Newcastle, Maine," (unpublished manuscript, 1980, 3) states that Glidden may have met Vaughan in England, perhaps through the artist John LaFarge.

2. "Consecration of S. Andrew's Church, Newcastle," *North East,* XI, December 1883, 45.

3. Geographical designations throughout are ecclesiastical, that is, east refers to the altar end of the church, etc.

4. The roof was originally covered with wood shingles; these have recently been replaced by rather unsympathetic green and red composition roofing. The timber framing has recently been restored to its original dark green.

5. Kempe did the east window at Melverley in 1879.

6. "S. Andrew's," *North East,* 45.

7. Ibid.

8. Rev. Maurice W. Venno, untitled pamphlet on St. Andrew's, 1959.

9. Betjeman, *An American's Guide,* 461.

10. For example, the ceiling of St. Michael's, Kingsland, Herefordshire (1886–1868), and the nave restoration of St. Mary's, Cheshunt, Hertfordshire (1874), as well as that done for Bodley by Morris in the Hall of Queens' College, Cambridge, in 1875. "Bodley's influence on Morris at this time can hardly be overemphasized. . . . Edward Warren, Bodley's pupil, says that Bodley himself actually designed one or two of Morris's early wallpapers" (Verey, "Bodley," 89).

An example of Vaughan's commitment to his art can be found in the stenciled ceiling of St. Andrew's Church in Newcastle, Maine. For this, his first parish church, Vaughan insisted that the nave and chancel ceiling be painted according to his designs. As the vestry was apparently unwilling to fund this work, Vaughan did it himself, spending an entire summer on his back, painting the ceiling.

11. Vaughan's interest in carving was more than academic, for his successor at the National Cathedral, Philip Hubert Frohman, remembered "that at the time Vaughan was practicing architecture he was the only man in America who could properly design a gothic *molded* capital. Numerous other gothicists could design a capital to include carving but they simply did not know how to correctly draw a molded one" (letter from Richard T. Feller, Clerk of the Works, Washington Cathedral, to author, December 2, 1969).

12. In his *Utopian Craftsmen,* Lionel Lambourne devotes a chapter to music in the Arts and Crafts Movement. For his organ cases Bodley (who was himself an organist) was assisted by Canon Frederick Sutton, author of *Church Organs, their Position and Construction* (1872). Sutton designed the cases for both Pendlebury and Hoar Cross (Verey, "Bodley," 93). Vaughan's patron, Edward Searles (see Chapter 6) was an organist and organ manufacturer, and Vaughan is well known among organ enthusiasts for his design of the Serlo Organ Hall in Methuen. The organ at St. Andrew's was installed in 1888.

13. St. James-the-Less is one of the most important ecclesiological churches in the history of the Gothic Revival in America and is featured in Phoebe Stanton's *The Gothic Revival and American Church Architecture.* Vaughan was consulted by J. T. Windrim on the design of the Wanamaker bell tower and mausoleum at St. James in 1908 (Stanton, 107), and Vaughan probably designed the church's 1907 organ case (replaced in 1928).

14. The Cowley Fathers' own conventual church outside Oxford, begun in 1894, was designed by Bodley. Brother Maynard, who worked in Bodley's office before he joined the Society, also did the ceiling paintings at Cowley, as well as the ceiling medallions at St. Margaret's Chapel. During the 1880s it was considered fashionable to entertain members of religious orders at one's summer place. Architect Halsey Wood and Florence Hemsley Cox were married at St. John in 1889.

15. Arthur Brown's *History of Penacook,* (Concord, 1902, 108) states that the rector of St. Paul's School, Henry Coit, donated the costs of the architect's fees and was undoubtedly responsible for the selection of Vaughan as the designer of St. Mary's. Brown further states that the lines of the church were drawn on that of "a church in Cornwall, England." This Cornish reference perhaps derives from the number of English stone cutters from Cornwall who lived in the north end of nearby Concord. This group of English immigrants was served by St. Timothy's Mission, a granite chapel built also at the instigation of the rector of St. Paul's. Now demolished, St. Timothy's was almost certainly designed by Vaughan; its altar was donated to the Church of the Holy Spirit in Plymouth, New Hampshire. The unusual conical roof treatment at Penacook is remarkably similar to dormers found on St. Mark's School in Southborough, Massachusetts, built in 1890. The English details of the half-timbered school suggest that its architect, Henry Forbes Bigelow, was an admirer of Vaughan and perhaps apprenticed with, or worked for Vaughan in the late 1880s. Bigelow is best known for his 1913 addition to the Boston Athenaeum.

16. St. Mary's, Dorchester (Boston) of 1887–1888 might also be included, for its magnificent timber roof is one of the finest of its kind in the U.S. St. Mary's is unusual in that it has a semi-octagonal apse; transepts were added by Hartwell & Richardson in 1893. For a more complete discussion of St. Mary's, see Douglass Shand Tucci, *The Gothic Churches of Dorchester,* Boston, 1974.

17. R. E. Armstrong, "The Church of the Holy Name, Swampscott," *Church Militant,* VII, October 1904, 121. Holy Name has been a year-round parish for many years.

18. Ibid. Some of the windows are later.

19. "When the Church was consecrated a wise request was made, viz., that no piece of furniture be placed in the chancel or nave without the approval of the architect" (ibid.).

20. The rectory cost $7,000 (Edward F. Tillotson, "The Swampscott Rectory," *Church Militant,* IX, April 1908, 7). St. Paul's, Gardner, Massachusetts (1909), another simple rectangular Vaughan design, was to have had a rectory for which Vaughan drew up plans ("a Mid-Victorian, three story rectory, with servants quarters, etc."), but it was not built (Canon Rush D. W. Smith to Canon A. Pierce Middleton, May 11, 1970). The design of the church at Gardner was for a granite structure to seat 275 people; the original drawings for the church are in the St. Paul's archives.

21. All Saints originally had stenciling on the walls. The rectory next door was a plain frame house that had been "Gothicized," undoubtedly by Vaughan, with the grafting of half-timbering onto the gable ends.

22. "The New Church at Methuen," *Church Militant,* VIII, October 1905, 10. The cornerstone was laid in 1904.

23. "Consecration at North East Harbor," *North East,* XXX, September 1902, 20–21. Bishop Doane was the son of the architecturally conscious Bishop George Washington Doane, for whom Richard Upjohn built St. Mary's, Burlington, N.J. (1846–1848), an early example of an American church based on actual English medieval sources. The younger Doane, a friend of Bishop Lawrence, was also noted for his Anglophilia and for his dream of joining all English-speaking churches. The rectors of both Groton (Endicott Peabody) and St. Paul's schools (Samuel Drury) summered at Northeast Harbor and it is likely that they influenced the choice of Vaughan as architect.

24. The residents of Beverly Farms ("there are in the summer more wealthy Church people than in any town in Massachusetts except Lenox") objected to having to worship at St. Peter's in the factory town of Beverly, but Bishop Phillips Brooks had dismissed the idea of a separate church as a "toy parish" (*Church Militant,* III, October 1900, 12). St. John's remained a chapel of St. Peter's until 1909.

25. St. John's cost $17,000 (*American Architect and Building News,* XCIII, February 26, 1908, 73). Originally, St. John's had a plan almost identical to that of All Saints, Methuen; this was altered in 1962 by the extension of the north aisle.

26. The cornerstone of St. Peter's Mission in the northern Vermont village of Lyndonville was laid on September 11, 1898 (*The Mountain Echo,* 5, October 1898). The October 1897 issue of the diocesan magazine carried an appeal for a church at Lyndonville and noted that a site had been given for both church and parsonage, with the latter already "in the course of erection." Another of Vaughan's small rural churches—and one of the most consciously picturesque—is Christ Church in the Berkshire village of Sheffield. Designed in 1910 (or possibly earlier) and built in 1912, Christ Church combines both seam-faced stone and half-timbering; the yellowish-brown stone is almost identical in color to that at St. John's, Beverly Farms. A watercolor rendering of Christ Church was published in *Church Militant,* XIII, December 1910, 7.

27. Henry Herbert Smythe, "St. Barnabas' Church, Falmouth," *Church Militant,* VII, October 1904, 112–113. A parish house, also the gift of the Beebe family, and which was undoubtedly by Vaughan, was built at the same time. A cloister was originally planned to connect church and parish house (Rev. Richard S. Crowell, interview, Falmouth, Mass., August 25, 1970). St. Barnabas has a fairly complete set of drawings for the church, as well as an "approved" plan for landscape design by Frederick Law Olmsted & Co., dated April 12, 1890.

28. The tower collapsed in a heavy storm during construction; the "tower and spire were re-erected, the proportions being changed and made heavier and higher" (Henry Herbert Smythe, "A History of St. Barnabas Parish," unpublished manuscript, St. Barnabas Memorial Church, Falmouth, Mass., n.d.). The tower was undoubtedly inspired by similar ones employed by Bodley, for example, All Saints, Jesus Lane, Cambridge (completed in 1870), and St. John, Tue Brook, Liverpool (1868–1870).

29. The use of stone was probably dictated by local preference; the stone in this case was procured from the nearby "quarry of W. E. Elder in the vicinity of Rochester" (*Souvenir Report of the Cost of Building the New St. Thomas' Church, Dover, N.H., n.d.*).

30. Interestingly, Voysey regarded himself as the "last remaining disciple of Pugin"

(David Gebhard, *Charles F. A. Voysey, Architect,* Santa Barbara, 1970, from the Introduction by John Brandon-Jones, 4). Voysey (1857–1941) was very much like Vaughan in temperament; both were extremely private men who worked virtually alone. While Voysey went beyond Vaughan in his insistence that "all objects surrounding him, even down to the smallest, should be the epitome of their type," both shared the total decoration concept of the Arts and Crafts Movement, and as indeed there is "something quite distinctive about going into a Voysey house," the same can be said about going into a Vaughan church (Duncan Simpson, *C. F. A. Voysey: An Architect of Individuality,* London, 1979, 17).

31. Louis W. Flanders, *A Short History of the Founding of St. Thomas' Church,* Dover, N.H., 1939, 9. One of the competition designs was entered by the new firm of Cram & Wentworth and is discussed in Ann Miner Daniel's doctoral dissertation on Cram (*The Early Architecture of Ralph Adams Cram, 1889–1902,* University of North Carolina, 1978, 114–116).

32. Vestry Records of St. Thomas' Church, Dover, N.H., Record No. 86, August 30, 1890, 196. Vaughan's commission for St. Thomas's was $1,195.35 (*Souvenir Report*). The "chapel" mentioned in the Vestry Records may refer to the morning chapel. However, Vaughan undoubtedly designed the Furber Memorial Chapel in Forest Glade Cemetery in the neighboring town of Somersworth. This simple, three-bay, granite chapel was donated by Lizzie Jane Poor in honor of her parents and erected in 1897. James Thomas Furber was General Manager for the Boston and Maine Railroad and maintained a summer home in Somersworth.

33. This problem of reconciling medieval plans with contemporary churchmanship is the topic of a research paper by Morgan W. Phillips, "Medievalism and Modern Needs in American Church Planning of the Eclectic Period," Columbia University, 1968. Phillips's example of successful compromise planning using narrow columns of wood or iron is Vaughan's St. John's, Beverly Farms.

34. Historical information on St. Martin's supplied by Margaret F. Barney from an untitled, undated manuscript on history of the church, compiled perhaps by Rev. Linden H. White about 1945.

35. Betjeman, *An American's Guide,* 81. Ralph Adams Cram's marriage to Elizabeth Carrington Reed took place at St. Martin's on September 20, 1900.

36. Herman Page, "The Consecration of Christ Church, Swansea," *Church Militant,* III, May 1900, 11. The final cost was closer to $35,000, with Mrs. Stevens making up the difference.

37. Lawrence, "Henry Vaughan," 4.

38. Quoted in *The Harvester* (September 11, 1971).

39. Richard T. Loring, "St. John's Church, Newtonville," *Church Militant,* VII, October 1904, 65.

40. "A New Church at Chestnut Hill," *Church Militant,* XVI March 1913, 6–7. This article gives Vaughan the middle initial of "G."

41. Ibid. Vaughan offered his plans free of charge, provided bids for construction were below $50,000. The bids were higher and in the Vestry Minutes for March 4, 1913, is the notation: "Add for architect's fees 6% on $87,000 . . . $5,430." The cornerstone was laid on November 24, 1913.

42. Church of the Redeemer, Vestry Minutes, January 6, 1914. The rector, Lucian W. Rogers, made it clear to the parish that the new church should be built so as to bestow "a blessing upon the community for all time," and asked for subscriptions to the "point of sacrifice" ("New Church at Chestnut Hill," 6).

43. Redeemer, Vestry Minutes, May 7, 1916; June 7, 1918.

44. There are very few English medieval parish churches that are pure examples of a single Gothic style, and Vaughan was perhaps trying to capture the flavor of an older church that has been added to in a later style by succeeding generations. However, given Vaughan's extensive knowledge of English Gothic it seems unlikely that he divided English Gothic into the artificial periodization that textbooks so often do (e.g., Perpendicular succeeding Decorated c. 1340), but rather understood and appreciated the subtleties of English Gothic's gradual evolution.

45. "New Church at Chestnut Hill," 6. It would not be unfair to ascribe laudatory platitudes to a bishop consecrating a new church in his diocese. However, it would be a mistake to dismiss Lawrence's championing of Vaughan as pious generalities. Lawrence not only shared Vaughan's admiration for English Gothic, he regarded it as an important factor in the consolidation of Episcopalianism in Massachusetts.

CHAPTER 3

1. E. Clowes Chorley, *Men and Movements in the American Episcopal Church,* New York, 1946, 351. The Order of the Holy Cross took its name from the mission church.

2. The English foundation was so unpopular with the Church of the Nativity that that parish decided to founder rather than accept the society's offer of union. Dr. William M. Hogue, Headmaster of the Tome School, Port Deposit, Md., and biographer of Fr. Huntington, shared his extensive knowledge of American religious orders with the author.

3. Fr. Sturgis Allen, "Reminiscences," unpublished manuscript, n.d., 58 (Order of the Holy Cross Archives, West Park, N.Y.)

4. St. John Baptist Foundation, *Report of the Work of the Sisters of St. John Baptist, in the German Mission of the Holy Cross . . . From Jan., 1883, to May, 1887,* New York, n.d. (O.H.C. Archives).

5. Letter from Rev. A. Appleton Packard, Archivist, Order of the Holy Cross, June 8, 1970.

6. Confirming their shared similarity of approach, the work closest to Holy Cross Church is Bodley's church for the Cowley Fathers in Oxford of a decade later.

171

7. In 1904 Vaughan designed the monastery for the Order of the Holy Cross at West Park, N.Y. (see Chapter 5).

8. St. Bartholomew's is now the First Holiness Apostolic Church of the True Faith. The tower was probably never built. The church has undergone considerable remodeling and little of Vaughan's work is recognizable.

9. Beginning in 1894 and lasting until about 1906, Vaughan made extensive additions to St. Mark's Church in Philadelphia, one of the great monuments of American Ecclesiology, designed by John Notman, 1847–1849 (see Stanton, *Gothic Revival,* 115–25). While this included erection of a cloister leading to the nave and some structural rebuilding of the foundations and flooring, most of Vaughan's work consists of decorative details: choir stalls, organ gallery, doors, and the rood (the rood beam and two of the doors are illustrated in advertisements for Irving & Casson in the *Magazine of Christian Art* in 1908). These modifications transformed what had been a rather severe—albeit High Church—building into a richly ornamented expression of Anglo-Catholicism. Constance Greiff, Director, Heritage Studies, Princeton, N. J., documented Vaughan's work at St. Mark's while preparing a catalogue on Notman for the Philadelphia Athenaeum in 1978.

10. A receipt in the Christ Church archives, dated 1896, notes that Vaughan was paid $3,871, or 5% of an outlay of $77,420, although the total cost was closer to $90,000 (Rev. William G. Kibitz, interview, New Haven, Ct., September 19, 1969). According to Fr. Kibitz (interview, April 6, 1981), the Christ Church commission came to Vaughan through his friendship with the rector, George Brinley Morgan. Morgan had previously been rector of Christ Church in Exeter, N.H., where Vaughan added stenciling sometime before 1887 (Christ Church, Exeter, was recently destroyed). Fr. Morgan was killed in 1908 when he was run over by an automobile in front of the church. Vaughan designed the 18-foot-high Indiana limestone memorial cross which was placed before the east window. The 1911 Swords Cross in the graveyard of Trinity Church in New York is so similar to the Morgan Cross as to suggest that it is by Vaughan.

11. An angel on the main entranceway to St. Swithun's (which was designed by Garner when Vaughan was still with Bodley & Garner) is reproduced as a drip molding by Vaughan on the tower of Christ Church, and is almost identical to that used on the tower parapet at the Redeemer.

12. Not all Magdalen-inspired towers were as successful as that at Christ Church. For example, William Appleton Potter's Church of the Divine Paternity in New York, of which the *Architectural Review* of June 1899 said: "This design well illustrates the want of feeling for Gothic Proportions which we have been deploring. The design of the tower is obviously founded on the glorious tower of Magdalen College, Oxford, but the architect seems not to have appreciated on what the beauty of the fifteenth century design depended." In the August issue of the same journal, Cram singled out Potter's church as an example of bad Modern Gothic ("Good and Bad Modern Gothic," 117). Potter's work at this time shows an interesting metamorphosis from an exuberant Ruskinian Gothic to a rather doleful academic version of English Tudor—best illustrated by his two adjoining libraries for Princeton University, Chancellor Green and East Pyne, built in 1873 and 1897, respectively.

13. Cram, *Church Building,* 77.

14. "Christ Church is proud to be a pioneer in the good work of abolishing the ugly and disfiguring boxes, or pens, called pews" (*Christ Church Chronicle*, X, December 1899).

15. Christ Church has several letters from Kempe concerning the windows. The east window was, in Vaughan's opinion, "the most beautiful one in this country" (*Christ Church Chronicle*, VIII, April 1898).

16. The stations, the reredos, and other stonework are by John Evans, while the pulpit, rood screen, confessional, and font are by Johannes Kirchmayer, chief carver for Irving & Casson. The font was exhibited at the World's Columbian Exposition in Chicago in 1893.

17. Good Shepherd became a separate parish in 1967. Actually named the Alfred Corning Clark Memorial Chapel of the Incarnation, the chapel was given by Edward Severin Clark in memory of his father (J. Newton Perkins, *History of the Parish of the Incarnation, New York City, 1852–1912*, Poughkeepsie, 1912, 204–205).

18. In more recent times, the improving quality of the neighborhood rendered such facilities obsolete, and the parish house was sold to a school in 1969. In 1904 Vaughan built a four-story granite parish house and rectory for St. Luke's in Baltimore. St. Luke's Church was built in 1847–1857 by Niernsee & Nielson and completed by J. W. Priest, an architect recommended by the New York Ecclesiological Society and one-time partner of H. M. Congdon (see Stanton, *Gothic Revival*, 298–301).

19. Rev. John R. McDonald, interview, New York, March 4, 1970. Good Shepherd is reputed to have the most perfect acoustics of any church in New York; Fr. McDonald had numerous requests to use the church for recording purposes; for example, Perry Como recorded the "Lord's Prayer" here.

20. During construction of Good Shepherd, Vaughan designed the Chapel of the Nativity in the parent Church of the Incarnation (1903). Separated from the rest of the church by a rich screen, this narrow morning chapel has a 10-foot chancel; its east wall is covered by a marble retable and reredos (featuring the Last Supper) by John Evans. The Chapel of the Nativity provides an interesting contrast with the barnlike and heavily decorated Victorian Gothic nave of the Incarnation by Emlen Littell (1856).

21. The tower appeared in the original blueprints but was not added until the 1920s. A darker stone, or even brick, would have given the church greater contrast and warmth. The site slopes downward toward the east end, and when viewed from that prospect, the chancel appears taller than the rest of the church, presenting a variation on the asymmetrical composition of tall chancel wall flanked by the lower morning chapel. The Church of the Mediator has blueprints for a rectory designed by Vaughan, presumably at the same time as the church. The house was to be half-timbered and its tall proportions and narrow oriel windows call to mind the work of Richard Norman Shaw. Vaughan was apparently one of three architects considered for the Chapel of the Intercession at 155th Street and Broadway and which was designed by the New York office of Cram, Goodhue & Ferguson in 1914.

22. Basic history and chronology of Washington Cathedral found in Richard T. Feller and Marshall Fishwick, *For Thy Great Glory* (Culpepper, Va.: 1965).

23. "Report of the Committee on the proposed Cathedral Building," May, 1906, 6–7. A certain "WASP" snobbery cannot be discounted in the Trustees' preference for English Gothic, as the Renaissance may have had connotations of Roman Catholicism as well as association with Italian immigrants. Also, St. Matthew's Cathedral (Heins & LaFarge, 1899) was in the "Italian" style.

24. "American churchmen are so weary of designs which glorify the originality of the architect . . . we long for pure Gothic" (Satterlee to Board of Trustees of Washington Cathedral, August 22, 1906). Satterlee's letter was written from Northeast Harbor, Maine.

25. Ibid. In addition to being associated with Liverpool, Bodley was working on designs for Grace Cathedral in San Francisco, as well as a cathedral in India, and had already built the cathedral in Hobart, Tasmania.

26. "Report of the Committee," 8.

27. Satterlee to Vaughan, October 8, 1906. Vaughan's almost curt reply shows modesty: "My only fear is that Mr. Bodley may object to having his name come last in the partnership" (Vaughan to Satterlee, October 10, 1908). Apparently Bodley and Vaughan agreed that Vaughan would be primarily an assistant until the older architect's imminent death, for as Bodley wrote to Satterlee (May 23, 1907) "Mr. Vaughan has been very retiring and very good . . . He will have plenty of work later on, I hope, in superintending the carrying out of the great cathedral" Charles H. Brent, *A Master Builder: Being the Life and Letters of Henry Yates Satterlee,* New York, 1916, 433–434. The southwest crossing pier of the cathedral, given by Elizabeth Stevens in 1927, is inscribed: "To the glory of God and in grateful memory of Henry Vaughan, First Architect of the Cathedral."

28. Vaughan stayed in England "about three months aiding Mr. Bodley" (Cathedral Minutes, October 29, 1907). In a photograph of the cornerstone-laying ceremony, Vaughan is seated between Theodore Roosevelt and J. P. Morgan (W. L. De Vries, *The Foundation Stone Book,* Washington, 1908, facing 108).

29. Vaughan to Satterlee, November 16, 1907.

30. Lloyd Hendrick to the National Cathedral Association, September 26, 1966. Mr. Hendrick later made a model from these drawings, but the scale was so small and incomplete that his plans for the model were "like making up for the first time working drawings of the exterior for the actual construction of the building." Hendrick further recalled having to "detail a great many parts of the project which had never been studied or designed, especially the transepts and west end."

31. The original plans are described in detail in an "Explanation of Preliminary Drawings Submitted by Architects Bodley and Vaughan in 1907" (Feller and Fishwick, *For Thy Great Glory,* Appendix B, 80–83). "I do not think that excess of richness is desirable, but rather much dignity and even solemn grandeur" (Bodley to Satterlee, January 31, 1907). An editorial in the *Architectural Review,* XIV, June 1907, 169, offered the following criticism: "Frankly speaking, the designs for the new Episcopal Cathedral in Washington are disappointing. Much was to be expected where there was no vexatious stipulations to hamper and embarrass the architects. It was hoped that

something would be thought out which would in some degree (if not more than that) characterize the American Episcopal Church of today. Possibly that could not be done. Possibly Fourteenth Century Gothic characterizes the American Episcopal Church of today, though we think not. From a totally different point of view, we indulged in the hope that something would be done, which, while not marking a new and modern epoch in architecture, might yet be a powerful architectural composition. The designs of the new cathedral show a fairly close copy of Canterbury Cathedral. Aside from the fact that a copy does not seem to be the thing for a national cathedral, it seems that this design is neither as impressive nor as monumental as such a church should be. The English cathedrals, surrounded by lawns and trees, hedgerows and smaller buildings, are interesting and picturesque, though seldom monumental—with the exception perhaps, of Lincoln. For monumental design, Trinity Church in Boston is far ahead of this copy of fourteenth-century English work." In his chapter on cathedrals in *Church Building,* Cram stated: "The Church has not changed, nor the requirements of a cathedral; nor, so far as we in this country are concerned, has the race been modified as to demand new modes of expression. The Church in England and her architectural style are our own, and no one can deprive us of our birthright" (p. 181).

32. The Bodley-Vaughan plan was later singled out by Cram in *Church Building* as the "ideal cathedral" (125). The cathedral dimensions were to be 476 feet long and 132 feet wide; the internal apex of the vaults was to be 93 feet above the nave floor.

33. This "massiveness of wall" and "sturdiness of pier" was noted by the succeeding architect who referred to it as "quite Norman" (Philip Hubert Frohman, "The Cathedral of St. Peter and St. Paul, Washington, D.C.," *American Architect,* CXXVII, April 22, 1925, 363). However, the sense of wall is typical of English medieval building from the Anglo-Saxon period until (and often including) the Perpendicular.

34. "The only criticism as yet which I or anyone has to find with the rest of the plans is that the west towers seem not to equal the rest" (Brent, *Master Builder,* 389). However, the cathedral designs were criticized in *The Magazine of Christian Art* of March 1908, both in an article by John Sutcliffe (291–298) and in an unsigned editorial, undoubtedly written by Cram (304–306).

35. Frohman's changes to the Bodley-Vaughan design are detailed in his "Report to the Cathedral Chapter, October 21, 1921" (Feller, Appendix C, 84–89). Later Frohman said: "Had Henry Vaughan lived, it is probable that he would have materially changed many of the unstudied features of the original design" (memorandum to Bishop James E. Freeman, June 15, 1942). Bishop Satterlee had expected Bodley's interior design to look like the architect's rejected plan for Liverpool Cathedral; however, the exterior "far exceeded" his expectations (Brent, *Master Builder,* 390).

36. "I am . . . going to make a judgmental statement about the five architects and each man's impact on the final product, the completed cathedral. I will suggest they rate in this order by their impact: Frohman, Bodley, Little, Vaughan, Robb" (letter from Richard T. Feller, Clerk of the Works, Washington Cathedral, March 27, 1974).

37. Vaughan to Satterlee, December 14, 1906. In this letter Vaughan also recommended Olmsted Bros. for the cathedral landscaping.

38. In 1912 Vaughan was also commissioned to design the Bishop's House in the

cathedral close. Constructed in 1913–1914, the Bishop's House is a three-story, H-plan, Elizabethan pile, complete with a private chapel with a polychromed wooden ceiling, as well as windows by Charles Connick. The Bishop's House is not dissimilar to the lodgings known as Bodley's Buildings which Vaughan's mentor erected at King's College, Cambridge, 1891–1894. In 1972 the Bishop's residence was converted into the diocesan headquarters.

39. Feller, 23.

40. After Vaughan's death, work was carried out by his head draftsman, Bussman; Frohman believed that it was Bussman who made "the mistake in the vaulting of our apse that had to be removed later" (letter from Feller, December 2, 1969). It is interesting to note some of the "Names of Architects Suggested for Washington Cathedral" (March 30, 1921): Bussman and John Elkhuysen (both of Vaughan's office, which Dean Bratenahl instructed Robert Casson to continue until successors could be found), Cram, Goodhue, Allen & Collens, Milton Medary, Frank Miles Day, Sir Ralph Lorimer (a pupil of Bodley), John Russell Pope, Cass Gilbert, Hobart Upjohn, and Russell Sturgis (Washington Cathedral, Bodley & Vaughan file).

41. Vaughan to Bishop Harding, May 7, 1914.

42. Although under terms of the original contract, the cathedral reserved the right to terminate its agreement upon the death of either partner, dismissal came as a bitter blow to the somewhat difficult La Farge. His design was viciously attacked on historical and aesthetic grounds in the anonymous "Candidus" letter in the *American Architect* (XCI, May 18, 1907, 203–204), which many believed to have been written by Cram. Speculation as to Cram's actual role in persuading the cathedral trustees to adopt Gothic (and hire Cram as architect) should be left to Cram's biographer. However, it is said that Cram "received severe professional censure for his interference" (John La Farge, *The Manner is Ordinary,* New York, 1957, 332). St. John the Divine is the subject of a doctoral dissertation by Janet Adams of Brown University; it is hoped that a book on the complex architectural history of St. John will result.

43. Letter from Lloyd Hendrick, January 27, 1970. Vaughan was one of fourteen architects invited to submit designs for the original competition for St. John, before the competition was opened to the architectural profession at large. In the Cathedral Archives there is Vaughan's letter of acceptance (June 30, 1888) and one to J. P. Morgan, Treasurer of the Cathedral Trustees (August 29, 1889) in which he regrets that pressures of other work kept him from preparing an entry.

44. Canon Edward N. West, Cathedral of St. John the Divine, interview, March 5, 1970.

45. Hendrick, interview with Feller, July 20, 1967. In agreeing to serve as consulting architect, Cram suggested the formation of an "Architectural Commission of the Cathedral of St. John the Divine" to consist of himself, La Farge, and Vaughan (Cram to Dean William M. Grosvenor, May 25, 1911). Such a commission may have been an attempt to placate men Cram considered as rivals. And while Cram wrote in a newspaper tribute to Vaughan that he and Vaughan worked together at St. John with a "singular sympathy and sense of cooperation" ("Masters in Architecture," *Boston Transcript,* July 20, 1917),

Cram was not known for his friendly relations with his fellow architects. Cram's tenure as consulting architect for Washington Cathedral after Vaughan's death was a stormy one and Frohman claimed that Cram had accused him of "taking the cream off the Cathedral profits" (Frohman to Cram, December 16, 1935).

46. Cram, *Church Building*, 300.

47. *Guide to the Cathedral of St. John the Divine*, New York, 1956, 146 ff. The remaining four chapels are the work of Carrère & Hastings, Cram, and Heins & La Farge.

CHAPTER 4

1. Waugh's school was Lancing College in Sussex, designed by Richard Cromwell Carpenter (1812–1855), one of the favorite architects of the Ecclesiological Society; the chapel was designed by his son, R. H. Carpenter.

2. A Chinese missionary visited the Church of the Redeemer in 1913. "He was asked what kind of parish church he had and he replied 'Oh! a beautiful stone church designed by your own architect, Mr. Henry Vaughan of Boston. . . . My church,' he said, 'is in a district surrounded by intelligent, well-to-do Chinese of the mandarin class. Would they be impressed if the place where "God's honour dwelleth" were inferior to a Buddist temple? Would they be convinced of the ideality and sincerity of my faith if my house of worship were less sightly than a government office, a municipal building, or even a railroad station? In case my church were built of bamboo, their comment would be "But you still keep your Saviour in the manger" ' " (William Blodgett, "Address on Building a New Church," Church of the Redeemer, March 9, 1913). Research has so far failed to locate this church, but it was probably a chapel for a school or college, presumably in Shanghai, or perhaps St. Paul's Cathedral in Hankow (1902).

3. Coolidge, "Gothic Revival," 225, 228. In *The Modern Princeton*, Princeton, 1947, Donald Drew Egbert referred to St. Paul's Chapel as the "first major example in the United States of this archaeologically more 'correct' Gothic" (90).

4. William Willard Flint, Jr., manuscript history of the chapel, St. Paul's School, 1933, (St. Paul's School Archives), 3. In an article titled "Good and Bad Modern Gothic," *Architectural Review*, (August 1899), Cram further stated: "In Henry Vaughan's Chapel at St. Paul's School we return from the dazzlingly personal to the reverently faithful, the thoughtful and scholarly spirit that varies from precedent only enough to give the work life and contemporaneousness. It has this in sufficient degree, and is in no respect archaeological, except in the sense that it is absolutely correct in detail . . . it shows admirably how close one can hold to medieval models and yet be thoroughly modern, thoroughly alive and real . . . Henry Vaughan's chapel is a model of calm composition, of self-respect" (117–118). Using an operatic analogy, Cram compared good Modern Gothic to Wagner's *Tristan* and bad to Verdi's *Traviata*.

5. "Henry Vaughan's Groton, St. Paul's and Cleveland chapels were the first school chapels and can never be altogether superseded so admirable are they in their quality" (Cram, *Church Building*, 308). The interior of St. Paul's, along with the exterior of Christ Church, New Haven, were illustrated in the official catalogue of the American fine arts exhibit at the Paris Exposition of 1900.

6. Ashburn, *Peabody of Groton,* 70. Bishop Grafton, a founder of the Cowley Fathers, was sent to America by Edward Pusey, a leader of the Oxford Movement; Vaughan designed Grafton's tomb in St. Michael's Chapel of St. Paul's Cathedral in Fond du Lac, Wisconsin. St. Paul's founder, Dr. George C. Shattuck, "a convert to Episcopalianism, was a moving spirit of Boston's Church of the Advent" (August Heckscher, *St. Paul's: The Life of a New England School,* New York, 1980, 34). "Charles Perkins Gardiner, of Brookline, came from the same background but brought to the board a sensitivity to the arts, especially to music and architecture. He introduced to the school the architect Henry Vaughan, whose touch was to be on the best of its older buildings" (ibid., 78). Mrs. George Shattuck was a patron of the House of the Good Samaritan in Boston (destroyed); the font in the chapel there was designed by Vaughan.

7. "The boarding school she sent him [Huntington Hartford] off to was not likely to insinuate much of the din of the outside world into his life. It was St. Paul's, which, like all the best eastern boarding schools, was a kind of country rector's Emersonian version of an English public school. The place was calcimined and bleached with the good odor of the 19th century sententiae and precepts concerning God, gentility, noblesse oblige and the virtues of active sport" (Tom Wolfe, *The Kandy-Kolored-Tangerine-Flake Streamlined Baby,* New York, 1965, 217). Heckscher (2–11) takes issue with the Eton model idea and discusses the educational philosophy of the founders and the Swiss and American schools they emulated. However, whatever the philosophy, the physical form, as represented by the chapel, is English "public school."

8. Ashburn, *Peabody,* 28.

9. Lawrence, "Henry Vaughan," 4. Almost three-quarters of a century later, it is perhaps tempting to be amused by Bishop Lawrence's sentiments. However, they were sincerely felt and could have just as easily been uttered by, say, Woodrow Wilson or J. P. Morgan.

10. *The Churchman,* 12, December 16, 1882, 678. Stevens was the benefactor of the Church of the Holy Innocents in Hoboken, designed by Edward Tuckerman Potter in 1874. Halsey Wood added the parish house in 1885 and a rectory in 1888. In 1895, Vaughan extended the nave and built a tower, sacristy, and choir room; Vaughan also designed the altar in the Lady Chapel. "American Catholic Parishes VII. Church of the Holy Innocents, Hoboken, N.J.," *Holy Cross Magazine,* XXIV, January 1913, 72–73.

11. Shinn, *Notable Episcopal Churches,* 222. The chapel building fund reached its goal of $100,000 by April 1886. "Like the cathedral builders of the Middle Ages, the little community found an objective for its efforts, a goal for its common strivings, in rearing stone upon sacred stone—while the rest of the world was rearing temples to Mammon" (Heckscher, *St. Paul's,* 103).

12. Another possible model is Pugin's chapel for St. Edmund's College (known as Old Hall Green Academy), Hertfordshire, completed in 1853. St. Paul's is like St. Edmund's in plan, in the use of materials, Decorated tracery, and especially in the proportional relationship of window to wall. Pugin designed a tower for St. Edmund's, but it was never built.

13. Coolidge, "Gothic Revival," 228. Coolidge goes on to say that "the most successful, the most personal, the most subtle, the most medieval [feature] is the remarkable

even emphasis on proportions, surface, and decoration. In this respect it is rivaled only by St. Mark's, Philadelphia."

14. Heckscher, *St. Paul's*, 218–220. "The late Charles Willing of Philadelphia, a distinguished architect and graduate of St. Paul's, told me that he refused to return to the School if the chapel were lengthened, on the grounds that you couldn't improve prefection, and Vaughan's original chapel was perfection itself in his mind" (letter from Matthew M. Warren, Rector Emeritus, St. Paul's, June 18, 1969). Later, the sacristy on the south wall of the chancel's first bay was extended outward by an addition, further detracting from Vaughan's unified plan.

15. The cloister, built of the same materials as the chapel, is a reasonably sympathetic addition, but its somewhat dry and less medieval design provides an interesting contrast between Vaughan and a leader of the Modern Gothic persuasion. When the cloister was added, a doorway was cut into the west side of the tower. Also in 1928, a chantry (which serves as baptistery and war memorial) was added to the north of the antechapel. The wooden entrance porch at Christ Church, Sheffield, is very similar to the original cloister at St. Paul's.

16. A typical reference is found in Samuel Chamberlain's *The New England Image*, New York, 1962, 96: "The brick Gothic chapel is reminiscent of rural England."

17. Coolidge, "Gothic Revival," 230.

18. The windows in the choir are all by Clayton & Bell and were installed between 1888 and 1915.

19. The present organ was built in 1930 and rebuilt in 1954 by the Aeolian-Skinner Co. of Boston, successors to Hutchings.

20. Cram, *Church Building*, 164. Never common in this country, perhaps the best-known example of a screen reredos is that at Cram & Goodhue's St. Thomas's Church, New York, done in 1917–1918; Lee Lawrie was the sculptor. For Kirchmayer see Douglass Shand Tucci, "A Carver of Saints—Johannes Kirchmayer," in *Germans in Boston*, Boston, 1981, 30–36.

21. Wells was evidently a rich source for Vaughan, and no doubt the Somerset cathedral featured in his illustrated lecture at the Church of the Advent in 1892.

22. Arthur Stanwood Pier, *St. Paul's School, 1855–1934* (New York: 1934), 212. Coit established an orphan's home in 1866 which occupied older structures just west of the school. However, a tall, brick, chapel-like building which appears in old photographs is obviously by Vaughan (illustrated in Heckscher, *St. Paul's*, 53).

23. Pier, *St. Paul's*, 214.

24. Ibid., 215. Clark is not mentioned in Pier's history. Nothing is known about this apparent collaboration with Clark (1853–1927), an architect who designed St. Ann's Church in Kennebunk, Me. (1887); Clark's designs for two Shingle Style houses in Kennebunkport of 1880 and 1882 may help explain Vaughan's one foray into domestic design in a similar style, the Thistles of 1888 (see Chapter 5; Clark's Maine houses were published in the *American Architect* and are illustrated in Vincent Scully's *The Shingle Style*, figs. 52–53). One of the leading proponents of the Shingle Style, William Ralph

Emerson also had his office at 5 Pemberton Square at this time.

25. "Structurally it was as sound as Gibraltar and just as inflexible . . . It was a monstrous thing from a contemporary point of view, but the boys loved living in it. It was a good place for young boys to be rough in, to make their squeally noises" (Matthew Warren to author, June 26, 1970). The Lower School was torn down in 1971.

26. Pier, *St. Paul's*, 269. The New Upper School was placed rather far away from the other school buildings upon the recommendation of Olmsted Bros., who drew up an overall plan for St. Paul's in 1898. The New Upper "showed that an uncertain client can be responsible for a good architect's producing a poor building. It possessed no visible entrance, no outward expression of the various dormitories and masters' apartments within, and—worst of all for students and faculty—no closets. (The architect was said to have 'forgotten' these, though he may have had in mind some form of medieval armoires). . . . A dining hall, rivaling the chapel in the beauty of its oak paneling and vaulted ceiling, crowned the work. That, at least, spoke for Vaughan at his best" (Heckscher, *St. Paul's*, 130). One clue to the missing closets may be found in a letter from Vaughan to Professor George T. Little of Bowdoin concerning the elevator in Hubbard Hall: "My boy who traced the plans must have omitted the lift, it certainly is shown on the drawing he traced from" (March 23, 1901, Bowdoin College, Special Collections).

27. The figure is for the estimate awarded to the Boston contractor, Woodbury & Leighton (Woodbury & Leighton to Vaughan, March 29, 1893), a firm that built a number of Vaughan buildings, including St. Paul's Chapel.

28. The Searles building came to Bowdoin largely through the efforts of Thomas H. Hubbard, a college trustee and law partner of Searles. Hubbard, as *de facto* donor, guided the building through design and construction. Hubbard's papers (Bowdoin College Archives) include a letter (on Southern Pacific Railroad stationery) dated March 31, 1893, to Vaughan concerning bids, costs, etc. When Searles was unable to attend the dedication ceremonies on September 20, 1894, Hubbard gave the "Address of Presentation for the Donor." Vaughan also designed the organ case for Grace Church, San Francisco, as a memorial to Mrs. Searles—just one of many works done for Searles (see Chapter 6).

29. *Address at the Dedication of the Mary Frances Searles Science Building, Bowdoin College,* Brunswick, Me., 1894.

30. Originally a yellow color (Bowdoin legend says that Searles owned the brickyard and specified the bricks), the building has been painted red for years. In a letter to Vaughan (April 5, 1893), Woodbury & Leighton suggested that costs could be cut by omitting buff brick and substituting "good common brick" (Bowdoin College Archives).

31. Minutes, Board of Trustees, Bowdoin College, June 26, 1894.

32. Charles T. Burnett, *Hyde of Bowdoin,* Boston, 1931, 168. Hubbard was also a chief financial backer of Robert E. Peary's polar expeditions; the Peary-MacMillan Arctic Museum is housed in Hubbard Hall. "I have specified everything to be the very best" (Vaughan to Professor Little, May 8, 1901, Bowdoin College, Special Collections).

33. Thomas H. Hubbard to William DeWitt Hyde, President of Bowdoin, March 30,

1900 (Bowdoin College, Hubbard papers). Bowdoin College Library has approximately sixty letters from Vaughan to Professor Little concerning the construction of Hubbard Hall. In the earliest of these (February 2, 1900), Vaughan says "I hope in the course of a day or two to send you a perspective view of the Library." The letters, which run until April 30, 1914, are remarkably brief and usually limited to one particular aspect of construction. With the exception of Vaughan's frequent apologies for delays, this correspondence is frustratingly unrevealing.

34. Louis C. Hatch, *History of Bowdoin College* (Portland, 1927), 432. Herbert R. Brown, Professor Emeritus of English at Bowdoin, tells the story of a Brunswick native who, as a little boy, remembers the construction of Hubbard Hall and specifically a woodcarver who worked all night in a shack set up on the building site. The details were more than he could handle easily, or had handled before, and was thus forced to work overtime on them (interview, September 23, 1969). Professor Brown lives in the Hubbard Hall apartment originally set aside for General Hubbard. The Rare Book Room on the second floor was designed by Grant La Farge and was originally the library of a New York mansion. The Hubbard Grand Stand, begun in the spring of 1903 and built at a cost of $30,180, is 122 feet long and 37 feet wide, with a steel frame, a fieldstone base, and brick walls. Dressing rooms and athletic storage facilities are beneath tiered seating for 580 people shielded from the elements by a hipped slate roof supported by six steel columns across the front and by brick buttresses on the sides and rear. A campus publication stated that the "grandstand will be the finest in the country until Harvard's new stadium is built and even then it will be the finest in proportion to its size. It will be constructed in the solid manner which marks all of Mr. Vaughan's buildings" (*Bowdoin Orient*, March 26, 1903, 271). While an unusual type of building for Vaughan, the Hubbard Grand Stand demonstrates the architect's ability to design utilitarian structures that are as handsome and as visually satisfying as his more historically inspired works.

35. "The late Librarian of Bowdoin, Gerald Wilder, once told me that Vaughan envisioned extending the stem of the 'T' and then crossing it with a wing to make the building have the form of an 'H' as a tribute to the donor . . . This plan was abandoned when it was decided to build a new library . . . Although I have never seen the plans, I recall Mr. Wilder saying that blueprints were drawn" (letter from Herbert R. Brown, September 18, 1969). There is a tradition of such "alphabet" structures, for example John Thorpe's "Design for a house based on the initials I.T." (John Summerson, *Architecture in Britain, 1530–1830,* rev. ed., Harmondsworth, 1977, Fig. 46). Hatch (*History of Bowdoin,* 432) and other sources refer to "Harvard" brick; another says "New Hampshire" brick.

36. Vaughan to Professor Little, November 1, 1901 (Bowdoin College, Special Collections).

37. Hatch, *Bowdoin,* 432; "Why Bowdoin is Proud of her Sons," *Sunday Herald* (Boston), September 30, 1917.

38. Montgomery Schuyler, "Architecture of American Colleges," *Architectural Record,* XXIX, February 1911, 156.

39. The first Groton Chapel is half-timbered and is similar to St. Andrew's, Newcastle. When the new chapel was built, the old one was given to the local Roman Catholic

parish and moved to the center of the village of Groton, where it still stands as the Chapel of the Sacred Heart. The exterior half-timbering has been painted white, as has the entire interior. J. P. Morgan was the treasurer of the Protestant Episcopal Church of the United States and was involved with the building of Washington Cathedral and St. John the Divine, as well as Groton. The Philadelphia architect, George Howe, was a student at Groton and recalled how he watched the Bishop of Massachusetts trip and fall in his eagerness to greet the financier and wondered if the cleric would have done the same had Jesus been visiting Groton (William F. Shellman, Professor of Architecture, Princeton University, Princeton, October 24, 1972).

40. Ashburn, *Peabody of Groton*, 90. That the chapel reinforced the impression of Groton as a school in the tradition of Thomas Arnold of Rugby strongly appealed to Peabody. The rector's cousin, Robert Swain Peabody, was the official school architect; however, as donor of both chapels, Gardner no doubt exercised some say in the choice of the designer.

41. The Diocese of Massachusetts, under Bishop Lawrence, was committed to English architecture but was (and still is) one of the "lowest" dioceses in the country, perhaps in deference to Puritan resistance to "popery." Although an American, Peabody himself was educated at Cheltenham and at Trinity College, Cambridge.

42. Groton Chapel has wonderful acoustics—for music at least; it is less satisfactory for preaching, which is perhaps a subtle comment on Vaughan's part. However, there is no reason to believe that Vaughan's acoustics, good or bad, were other than accidental.

43. William Amory Gardner, "Groton School, Groton," *Church Militant*, VII October 1904, 128–129.

44. Samuel Mather, "The Amasa Stone Memorial Chapel," Dedicatory Address, June 13, 1911, Case Western Reserve University Archives. John Hay's—and thus Clara Stone Hay's—friendship with Henry Adams may have been an influence in the choice of Vaughan (and the Gothic style) for the Western Reserve commission. Adams's book *Mont-Saint-Michel and Chartres* (Boston, 1905) was one of the cultural touchstones of Boston Gothicists and symbolized the philosophical reaction to the age of Marx, Spencer, and Bismarck. Cram wrote the introduction to *Mont-Saint-Michel*.

45. This figure is the book value given by an insurance company in 1919. "It was their custom to carry buildings at the cost of construction" (letter from Ruth W. Helmuth, Archivist, Case Western Reserve University, May 7, 1969). "Unfortunately, the University Archives does not contain very much material on Amasa Stone Chapel since the building was the gift of Amasa Stone's daughters and apparently all of the financial and business transactions were arranged by the family."

46. William E. Curtis, "Chapel Erected as Fit Memorial to Amasa Stone," *The Recorder-Herald* (Cleveland), June 14, 1911.

47. The whole exterior of Stone Chapel, exclusive of the tower, but including the clerestory windows and buttresses, is very much like Bodley's St. Michael, Camden Town, of 1876–1881, for which a tower was designed but never built.

48. Mather, "Stone Memorial Chapel."

gational Church in Great Barrington. It was built under Searles's supervision in 1883–1884, and if it was designed by Vaughan, it is likely that he was responsible for the Marigold and the coachman's quarters of the previous year. The Congregational manse (which is built of monochromatic gray masonry) and the carriage house feature prominent Romanesque arches (perhaps placing Vaughan in Richardson's office at this time). The two structures at Kellogg Terrace were also constructed of random ashlar, but they have darker stone window surrounds and horizontal accent stripes (as used later at Stanton Harcourt and at St. Barnabas Church), as well as Queen Anne detailing. The Great Barrington estate also has a hexastyle Roman Doric garden temple which was undoubtedly designed by Vaughan. Recalling eighteenth-century English landscape practice, the temple served as both teahouse and as part of a picturesque composition.

3. The organ was built in Boston by Searles's friend James E. Treat; constructed between 1886 and 1888, the three-manual organ with gold moldings was "declared by experts to be the most costly and effective instrument in private hands in this country" (*The Organ,* March 1894, 247). A description carried in the *New York Times* ("Millions in a Mansion," March 24, 1889, 13) calls the organ "the finest house organ in America." The instrument was later removed to Methuen and is now in the First Congregational Church there.

4. " 'But I have no connection with Bowdoin,' said Mr. Searles. 'What reason is there for my doing this?' 'Oh, give it in memory of your wife,' said the General" (Hatch, *History of Bowdoin,* 459). Hubbard's New York law firm, Butler, Stillman & Hubbard, handled Mrs. Hopkins's financial affairs from 1887; Searles was a silent partner in the firm.

5. Built in 1893, the organ (and choir stalls, also designed by Vaughan) was destroyed along with the church in the 1906 earthquake and fire. Bodley was hired to design a replacement (with C. G. Hare as his partner), but upon his death the commission for Grace Cathedral was given to Lewis P. Hobart of San Francisco. "The carving is well along and will suit you. It is pure Gothic—nothing else. Mr. Vaughan is at home with it, and the design carried me back to the land of many fine Organ cases, with those of Sir Gilbert Scott of which you are no doubt familiar" (James E. Treat to Searles, June 25, 1893, quoted in *Boston Organ Club Newsletter,* vol. 3, December 1967, 4). In *The Searles Saga* there is an illustration of an organ "donated to Westminster Abbey" by Searles (p. 88), but it is in fact that in Trinity Church in New York of about 1847.

6. Pine Lodge is now the Provincial House of the Sisters of the Presentation of Mary and is not open to visitors.

7. Flinton, *Searles Saga,* 128 (no source is given).

8. Mrs. Searles was buried in the 1891 Searles tomb (also designed by Vaughan) in the town cemetery; stylistically, the chapel is close to the Redeemer and the Mediator, and actually was completed in 1918. It is not dissimilar to Bodley's St. Mary's, Eccleston, of 1902 and is reminiscent of Bodley's own stiffer, more formal late manner.

9. De Lue, "Mystery Millionaire," 58.

10. There is a photograph of Sawgrist Hall in *Searles Saga,* p. 87. The factory burned in 1943.

11. William King Covell, "The Old Boston Music Hall Organ," *Old-Time New England,* 18 (April 1928), 185.

12. Richard M. Fremmer, "Edward F. Searles, Millionaire," unpublished manuscript, 1948, Nevins Memorial Library, 22. The "serf's cottage," known as "Meadow Brook Lodge," was probably the earliest building at Stillwater, erected c. 1896. Searles also erected a wooden house nearby called "Westmoreland Lodge," c. 1897 (Edgar Gilbert, *History of Salem, New Hampshire,* Concord, N.H.: 1907, 396).

13. A structural report on the Town Hall was made by the Society for the Preservation of New England Antiquities in the mid-1970s. "I don't recall that the report tells much, if anything about Vaughan's involvement with the building, but it does show what changes were made to the structure in the course of a 'medievalizing' remodelling which is still quite evident in the building. I had occasion to visit the building two years ago with Abbott Cummings, and he was dumbfounded to see, in the exposed roof trusses, what appeared to be the survival of rare seventeenth-century practices. On closer inspection with the help of ladders, we surmised that much of the antiquity we were seeing was actually clever late-nineteenth-century work. I immediately suspected Vaughan" (James L. Garvin, Curator, New Hampshire Historical Society, February 20, 1981).

14. W. S. Harris, *The News Letter* (Exeter, N.H.), November 9, 1906.

15. Ibid., February 5, 1909.

16. Oxfordshire Rural Community Council, *Historic Oxfordshire* (Oxford: 1951), 59–60 (the parsonage at Stanton-Harcourt is an "example of a building between the Jacobean and more formal classical style"). See also T. J. Goddard-Fenwick, *Stanton-Harcourt: A Short History,* 2nd ed. (n.p.: 1967).

17. Ruth L. Barnard, "Stanton Harcourt or Searles Castle of Windham, New Hampshire" (high-school term paper, 1955), Nesmith Library, Windham, N.H., 2. A trip for this sole purpose seems unlikely considering that Vaughan had already designed much of Pine Lodge and given his knowledge of English Gothic. But Vaughan went to Europe for a holiday in the summer of 1905 (spending three weeks in England and three in Italy) and he did visit England in 1907 to confer with Bodley about Washington Cathedral. Ronald Vaughan remembered his uncle visiting England to "study Gothic architecture" around 1906 (interview, October 6, 1970).

18. Barnard, "Stanton Harcourt," p. 2. The woodwork is almost certainly by Irving & Casson. Built on an 8-foot foundation that goes down to bedrock, the castle has an elaborate heating system with two furnaces, brass pipes that cost $12 a foot, copper drains, and silver-plated bathroom fixtures (undated broker's prospectus, F. M. & T. E. Andrew, Lawrence, Mass.). Stanton Harcourt was undoubtedly the model for Peyton's Castle, the sinister granite landmark that overlooked the town in Grace Metalious's best-selling novel *Peyton Place.* The author was from nearby Manchester and in the book one of her characters declares: "Every stick and stone, every doorknob and pane of glass in the castle was imported from England . . . I'd be willing to bet that this here is the only real, true, genuwine castle in New England" (Metalious, *Peyton Place,* New York, 1956, 331).

19. For a discussion of Mercer and his work, see William Morgan, "Henry Chapman

Mercer," *Harvard Bulletin* (August 1970), 27–29. Both Mercer and Vaughan were awarded silver medals at the Louisiana Purchase Exposition in St. Louis in 1904.

CHAPTER 7

1. Emerson, "Henry Vaughan," 286.

2. Slattery, "American Faces," 175–176.

3. Emerson, "Vaughan," 286.

4. In his *Church Building in Boston,* Douglass Shand Tucci deals with Vaughan's influence on Cram at some length. ". . . Vaughan was too modest to have been the artistic cutting edge of a militant Anglo-Catholicism, but by introducing him to the last phase of the English Gothic Revival (by then decisively Anglican) I think Vaughan had 'programmed' Cram, as it were, so that when, in 1886, he went again to Europe he was almost bound to draw certain crucial and now explicitly *religious* conclusions" (p. 93). "Vaughan made it impossible for Cram to ignore the fact that, however otherwise suspect, the new forces of the Oxford Movement in the Church of England, *and increasingly in America,* were apparently *the only impulses working towards the revival of recognizably Catholic art*" (p. 94).

BIBLIOGRAPHY

The Bibliography documents materials that mention Henry Vaughan and discuss buildings by him, as well as related material on George Frederick Bodley and some general background sources.

BOOKS, CATALOGUES, AND PAMPHLETS

Addison, James Thayer, *The Episcopal Church in the United States 1789–1931,* New York: 1951.

Addleshaw, George W. O., and Etchells, Frederick, *The Architectural Setting of Anglican Worship: An Inquiry into the Arrangements for Public Worship in the Church of England from the Reformation to the Present Day,* London: 1956.

Addresses at the Dedication of Hubbard Hall, the Library of Bowdoin College, Brunswick, Me.: 1903.

Addresses at the Dedication of the Jonathan Bourne Memorial Library, New York: 1897.

Addresses at the Dedication of the Mary Frances Searles Science Building, Bowdoin College, Brunswick, Me.: 1894.

Albright, Raymond W., *A History of the Protestant Episcopal Church,* New York: 1964.

Alexander, Donald Nelson, *History of the Diocese of Western Massachusetts,* Springfield, Mass.: 1951.

American Federation of Arts, *Art in Our Country,* Washington: 1923.

Anson, Peter F., *Fashions in Church Furnishings 1840–1940,* London: 1960.

Ashburn, Frank D., *Peabody of Groton,* 2nd ed., Cambridge, Mass.: 1967.

Bearse, Ray (ed.), *Vermont: A Guide to the Green Mountain State,* 2nd ed. rev., Boston: 1966.

Bloodgood, Edith Holt (ed.), *First Lady of the Lighthouse: A Biography of Winifred Holt Mather,* New York: 1952.

Brent, Charles H., *A Master Builder: Being the Life and Letters of Henry Yates Satterlee,* New York: 1916.

Brinkler, Alfred, *The Cathedral Church of Saint Luke: A History of Its First Century,* Portland: 1967.

Brown, David Arthur, *History of Penacook,* Concord, N.H.: 1902.

Brown, Herbert Ross, *Sills of Bowdoin: The Life of Kenneth Charles Morton Sills 1879–1954,* New York: 1964.

Burnett, Charles T., *Hyde of Bowdoin: A Biography of William De Witt Hyde,* Boston: 1931.

Burrage, Henry S., *Thomas Hamlin Hubbard*, Portland: 1923.

Cameron, Kenneth Walter (ed.), *Historical Resources of the Episcopal Diocese of Connecticut*, Hartford: 1966.

Catir, Norman Joseph, Jr., *St. Stephen's Church in Providence: The History of a New England Tractarian Parish 1839–1964*, Providence: 1964.

Chorley, E. Clowes, *Men and Movements in the American Episcopal Church*, New York: 1946.

Church, R. W., *The Oxford Movement*, Chicago: 1970.

Clark, Kenneth, *The Gothic Revival*, Harmondsworth: 1962.

Clarke, Basil F. L., *Anglican Cathedrals Outside the British Isles*, London: 1958.

───── , *Church Builders of the Nineteenth Century: A Study of the Gothic Revival in England*, rev. ed., New York: 1969.

Cole, David, *The Work of Sir Gilbert Scott*, London: 1980.

Consecration of S. Barnabas' Memorial Church, Boston: 1890.

Cram, Ralph Adams, *American Church Building of Today*, New York: 1919.

───── , *Church Building*, Boston: 1914.

───── , *The Gothic Quest*, New York: 1907.

───── , *My Life in Architecture*, Boston: 1936.

Crook, J. Mordaunt, *William Burges and the High Victorian Dream*, London: 1981.

De Vries, W. L., *The Foundation Stone Book*, Washington: 1908.

Diocese of Maine, Gardiner, Me.: 1920.

Dixon, Roger, and Muthesius, Stefan, *Victorian Architecture*, London: 1978.

Fawcett, Jane (ed.), *Seven Victorian Architects*, London: 1976.

Federal Writers Project, *Connecticut: A Guide to Its Roads, Lore, and People*, Boston: 1938.

───── . *Maine: A Guide Down East*, Boston: 1937.

Feller, Richard T., and Fishwick, Marshall W., *For Thy Great Glory*, Culpepper, Va.: 1965.

Fiftieth Anniversary of the Foundation of St. Mary's Parish, Dorchester, 1847–1897, Boston; 1898.

Flanders, Louis W., *A Short History of the Founding of St. Thomas' Church, Dover, N. H.*, p.: 1938.

Flinton, Martina, *The Searles Saga*, n.p.: 1976.

Frank S. Stevens Public Library Building, Fall River: 1901.

Gardner, William Amory, *Groton Myths and Memories*, Concord, N.H.: 1928.

Gilbert, Edgar, *History of Salem, New Hampshire*, Concord, N.H.: 1907.

Goody, Marvin E., and Walsh, Robert P. (eds.), *Boston Society of Architects: The First Hundred Years, 1867–1967*, Boston: 1967.

H. H. Richardson and His Office: Selected Drawings, Exhibition catalogue (Harvard University), Cambridge: 1974.

Harrington, Ty, *The Last Cathedral*, Englewood Cliffs: 1979.

Hatch, Louis C., *The History of Bowdoin College*, Portland: 1927.

Heckscher, August, *St. Paul's: The Life of A New England School*, New York: 1980.

Historic American Buildings Survey, *Maine Catalog*, Augusta: 1974.

Hitchcock, Henry-Russell, *The Architecture of H. H. Richardson and His Times*, rev. ed., Cambridge, Mass.: 1966.

Howard, F. E., *Medieval Styles of the English Parish Church*, London: 1936.

───── , and Crossley, F. H., *English Church Woodwork: A Study in Craftsmanship during the*

Medieval Period A.D. 1250–1550, London: 1917.

Howell, Peter, *Victorian Churches,* RIBA drawing series, London: 1968.

Jordy, William H., and Monkhouse, Christopher P., *Buildings on Paper: Rhode Island Architectural Drawings 1825–1945,* Providence: 1982.

Kowsky, Francis R., *The Architecture of Frederick Clarke Withers and the Progress of the Gothic Revival in America After 1850,* Middletown: 1980.

Lambourne, Lionel, *Utopian Craftsmen: The Arts and Crafts Movement from the Cotswolds to Chicago,* Salt Lake City: 1980.

Lawrence, L. W. [Mrs.], *The History of Searles Mansion,* Great Barrington: 1954.

Loth, Calder, and Sadler, Julius Trousdale, Jr. *The Only Proper Style: Gothic Architecture in America,* Boston: 1975.

Lyford, James O., *History of Concord New Hampshire,* Concord: 1903.

Lyon, Josephine A., *The Chronicle of Christ Church,* New Haven: 1941.

Memorials in St. John's Chapel, Groton School, Groton, Mass.: 1953.

Meynell, Mary, *The Church of the Holy Angels Hoar Cross,* Burton-on-Trent: 1966.

Muccigrosso, Robert, *American Gothic: The Mind and Art of Ralph Adams Cram,* Washington: 1980.

Muthesius, Stefan, *The High Victorian Movement in Architecture, 1850–1870,* London: 1972.

New York Association for the Blind, *Sixth Report of the New York Association for the Blind,* New York: 1912.

Oliver, Richard, *Bertram Grosvenor Goodhue,* New York: 1983.

Osterweis, Rollin G., *Three Centuries of New Haven, 1638–1938,* New Haven: 1953.

Parkinson, James, and Ould, E. A., *Old Cottages, Farmhouses and Other Half-Timber Buildings in Shropshire, Hereford, and Cheshire,* London: 1905.

Perkins, J. Newton, *History of the Parish of the Incarnation New York City 1852–1912,* Poughkeepsie: 1912.

Pier, Arthur Stanwood, *St. Paul's School, 1855–1934,* New York: 1934.

Pierson, William H., Jr., *American Buildings and Their Architects: Technology and the Picturesque,* New York 1978.

Roth, Leland M., *A Concise History of American Architecture,* New York: 1979.

———, *The Architecture of McKim, Mead & White, 1870–1920: A Building List,* New York: 1978.

Saint Andrew's Church, Newcastle, Maine: Consecration Service, Boston: 1883.

St. John Baptist Foundation, *Report of the Work of the Sisters of St. John Baptist in the German Mission of the Holy Cross,* New York: 1887.

Satterlee, Henry Y., *The Building of a Cathedral,* New York: 1901.

Scully, Vincent, Jr., *The Shingle Style and the Stick Style,* rev. ed., New Haven: 1971.

Service, Alistair, *Edwardian Architecture,* London: 1977.

Shinn, George Wolfe, *King's Handbook of Notable Episcopal Churches in the United States,* Boston: 1889.

Simpson, Duncan, *C. F. A. Voysey: An Architect of Individuality,* London: 1979.

Slattery, Charles Lewis, *Certain American Faces,* New York: 1918.

Souvenir Report of the Cost of Building the New St. Thomas' Church, Dover, N.H., April 3, 1893, n.p.: n.d.

Stanton, Phoebe B., *The Gothic Revival and American Church Architecture: An Episode in Taste 1840–1856,* Baltimore: 1968.

Tucci, Douglass Shand, *Built in Boston: City and Suburb, 1800–1950,* Boston: 1978.

_____ , *Church Building in Boston, 1720–1970,* Concord: 1974.

_____ , *The Gothic Churches of Dorchester,* Ann Arbor: 1974.

_____ , *Ralph Adams Cram, American Medievalist,* Boston: 1975.

Victorian Church Art, Exhibition catalogue, Victoria & Albert Museum, London: 1971.

White, James F., *The Cambridge Movement, the Ecclesiologists and the Gothic Revival,* Cambridge: 1962.

[Wood, Florence Hemsley], *Memories of William Halsey Wood,* Philadelphia: 1938.

Wright, Otis Olney, *History of Swansea, Massachusetts 1667–1917,* Fall River: n.d.

PERIODICALS

"A Massachusetts Palace," *New York Times,* July 6, 1891, 6.

"A Memorial Pulpit," *Church Militant,* XII, November 1909, 11.

"A New Block Island Mansion," *New York Times,* June 4, 1889, 3.

American Art Annual, XIV, 1917, 328.

"American Catholic Parishes, VII. Church of the Holy Innocents, Hoboken, N.J.," *Holy Cross Magazine,* XXIV, January 1913, 71–74.

Armstrong, R. E., "The Church of the Holy Name, Swampscott," *Church Militant,* VII, October 1904, 121.

Barton, George Edward, "Henry Vaughan," *AIA Journal,* 5, 1917, 518–519.

"Bethlehem Chapel," *Architecture and Building,* 44, 1912, 407–412.

Blackall, C. H., "Henry Vaughan," *American Architect,* CXII, July 11, 1917, 31.

Boston Organ Club Newsletter 3, December, 1967, 1–6.

Brickbuilder, VI, April, 1897, 86.

"Burial of Henry Vaughan: Famous Cathedral Architect Laid to Rest in Bethlehem Chapel Vault," *Washington Post,* November 2, 1917.

"Buried in a Vault under P. E. Chapel: Body of the late Henry Vaughan, Architect, Is Interred with Ceremony," *Evening Star* (Washington), November 2, 1917.

Cambridge Tribune, March 5, 1892.

Cheney, Robert F., "A Parish House for St. Paul's Church, Gardner," *Church Militant,* XII, April 1909, 8.

Christ Church Chronicle 4–5, July 1894 to January 1895.

Church Militant, 3, October 1900, 12.

Churchman, 12, December 16, 1882, 678.

"Consecration at North East Harbor," *North East,* 30, September 1902, 20–21.

"Consecration of St. Andrew's Church, Newcastle," *North East,* 11, December 1883, 44–45.

Covell, William King, "The Old Boston Music Hall Organ," *Old-Time New England,* XVIII, April 1909.

Cram, Ralph Adams, "Good and Bad Modern Gothic," *Architectural Review,* VI, August 1889, 115–119.

_____ , "Masters in Architecture—Langford Warren, Henry Vaughan," *Boston Transcript,* July 2, 1917.

Curtis, William E., "Chapel Erected as Fit Memorial to Amasa Stone," *Record-Herald* (Cleveland), June 14, 1911.

De Lue, Willard, "Methuen's Mystery Millionaire One of America's Strangest Men," *Boston Sunday Globe*, August 15, 1920.

Emerson, David B., "Henry Vaughan—An Appreciation," *Architectural Record*, 42, 1917, 286.

Field, C. N., "The Society of Saint Margaret," *Church Militant*, XII, February 1909, 8–9.

"First Episcopal Monastery: Holy Cross on the Hudson, Ceremoniously Blessed," *New York Sun*, May 20, 1904.

Frohman, Philip Hubert, "The Cathedral of St. Peter and St. Paul, Washington, D.C.," *American Architect*, 127, April 22, 1925, 355–368.

Gardner, William Amory, "Fifteen Years of Groton," *Church Militant*, III, April 1900, 5–6.

———— , "Groton School, Groton," *Church Militant*, VII, October 1904, 128–129.

"George Frederick Bodley," *Architect & Contract Reporter*, 78, October 25, 1907, 258–259.

Green, Margaret, "The Man Who Spent Mark Hopkin's [sic] Money," *Yankee*, March 1956, 51–55.

Harris, W. S., "Windham," *News Letter* (Exeter, N.H.), various issues 1904 to 1911.

Harrison, Hartley, "Millionaire of Methuen Was Too Often Misunderstood," *Sunday Herald* (Boston), September 12, 1920.

"Hubbard Hall, Bowdoin's Beautiful Library Building," *Portland Sunday Times*, June 14, 1903.

Huiginn, E. J. V., "St. John's Church, Beverly Farms," *Church Militant*, VII, October 1904, 116.

Jordan, Robert Paul, "House of Prayer for All People," *National Geographic*, 157, April 1980, 552–573.

Kernan, Michael, "Philip Hubert Frohman: A Lifetime Spent in Profound Revision," *Cathedral Age*, XLV, Winter 1970, 9–10.

Lawrence, William, "Henry Vaughan," *Church Militant*, XX, October 1917, 4.

"Likes to Beautify. Mr. Edward F. Searles Has Done Much for Town of Methuen," *Sunday Herald* (Boston), July 1, 1899.

Loring, Richard T., "St. John's Church, Newtonville," *Church Militant*, VII, October 1904, 65.

McGuire, George Alexander, "The Revival of St. Bartholomew's," *Church Militant*, XI, October 1908, 12.

"Memorial to the late G. F. Bodley," *Architectural Review*, 30, 1911, 101–102.

"Millions in a Mansion," *New York Times*, March 24, 1889, 13.

"Monastery Dedicated," *New York Daily Tribune*, May 20, 1904.

Morgan, William, "Addenda to Henry Vaughan: St. Mary's Church, Penacook," *Historical New Hampshire*, XXIX, Fall 1974, 187–189.

———— , "The Architecture of Henry Vaughan and the Episcopal Church," *Historical Magazine of the Protestant Episcopal Church*, XLII, June 1973, 125–135.

———— , "Henry Vaughan: An English Architect in New Hampshire," *Historical New Hampshire*, XXVIII, Summer 1973, 120–140.

———— , "Henry Vaughan: Cathedral Architect," *Cathedral Age*, XLVIII, Fall 1973, 18–19.

"The New Church," *Cowley Evangelist*, February 1894, 18.

"New Church at Chestnut Hill," *Church Militant*, XVI, March 1913, 6–7.

"New Church at Methuen," *Church Militant*, VIII, October 1905, 9–10.

"The New Grandstand," *Bowdoin Orient*, 32, March 26, 1903, 271–272.

New York Times, July 1, 1917, obituary page.

Oliphant, Charles H., "Methuen, Massachusetts," *New England Magazine*, XXIII, September 1900, 75–115.

Page, Herman, "The Consecration of Christ Church, Swansea," *Church Militant*, III, May 1900, 11.

Page, John Mitchell, "An Architect's Appreciation," *Holy Cross Magazine*, XIV, February 1903, 64–66.

Peabody, Endicott, "The Aim of Groton School," *Church Militant*, III, April 1900, 3–4.

Pease, Z. W., "The Bourne Whaling Museum," *Old Dartmouth Historical Sketch No. 44*, April 1916.

"School of Mr. Norman Shaw and Mr. Bodley," *Journal of the Royal Institute of British Architects*, 22, December 1900, 90–91.

Schuyler, Montgomery, "Architecture of American Colleges," *Architectural Record*, XXIV, February 1911, 145–166.

Simpson, Frederick Moore, "George Frederick Bodley," *RIBA Journal*, 15, (1907–1908), 145–158.

Smythe, Henry Herbert, "St. Barnabas' Church, Falmouth," *Church Militant*, VII, October 1904, 1.

Stavridi, Margaret, "Charles Eamer Kempe, Church Decorator for England, America and the World," *Stained Glass*, 74, Winter 1979–1980, 315–320.

Stearns, Foster W., "A New Church for Sheffield," *Church Militant*, XIII, December 1910, 7.

Sutcliffe, John, "The Washington Cathedral," *Magazine of Christian Art*, March 1908, 291–298.

Tillotson, Edward, "The Swampscott Rectory," *Church Militant*, April 1908, 6–7.

Tucci, Douglass Shand, "A Carver of Saints: Johannes Kirchmayer, America's Foremost Architectural Sculptor in Wood," *Germans in Boston*, 1981, 30–36.

Turner, William H., "St. Mary's Church Dorchester," *Church Militant*, VII, October 1904, 71.

"Two New Churches in the Diocese." *Church Militant*, V, March 1902, 2.

Vaughan, Henry, "The Late George Frederick Bodley, R.A., An Appreciation." *Architectural Review*, 14 (1907), 213–215.

"Vaughan Interred in Cathedral He Designed." *Washington Times*, November 2, 1915.

"War Memorial Dedicated." *Church Militant* 23, December 1920, 10.

Warren, Edward P. "George Frederick Bodley, R.A." *Architectural Review*, 2, 1902, 130–139.

———. "The Late George F. Bodley, R.A." *Architectural Review*, 22, November 1907, 230–231.

———. "The Work of Messrs. G. F. Bodley & T. Garner." *Architectural Review*, 6, 1899, 25–34.

"What Searles Did to Beautify Methuen," *Boston Herald*, September 26, 1920.

UNPUBLISHED MATERIALS

"A Successor to the Apostles Founds a Parish," manuscript, St. Mary's Church, Northeast Harbor, Me., n.d.

Allen, Sturgis, "Reminiscences," manuscript, Order of the Holy Cross, West Park, N.Y., n.d.

Baker, Benjamin, "The Jonathan Bourne Office and Some of Those Connected With It," manuscript, Old Dartmouth Historical Society, New Bedford, Mass., 1925.

Barnard, Ruth L, "Stanton-Harcourt or Searles Castle of Windham, New Hampshire," manuscript, Nesmith Library, Windham, 1955.

Black, George A. [Mrs.], "A Brief History of St. Paul's Parish, Gardner, Massachusetts," manuscript, St. Paul's Church, c. 1957.

Blodgett, William, "Address on Building a New Church," manuscript, Church of the Redeemer, Chestnut Hill, Mass., 1913.

Bowdoin College, Minutes of the Board of Trustees, 1894.

Christ Church (New Haven, Conn.), Minutes of the Vestry, 1886–1913.

Church of the Redeemer (Chestnut Hill, Mass.), Minutes of the Vestry, 1911–1920.

Coggeshall, Susanna, "A Brief History of St. Andrew's Parish in Newcastle, Maine," manuscript, 1980.

Coolidge, John P., "Gothic Revival Churches in New England and New York," thesis, Harvard College, 1935.

Daniel, Ann Miner. "The Early Architecture of Ralph Adams Cram, 1889–1902." Ph.D. dissertation, University of North Carolina, 1978.

"The Episcopal Church in Gardner: A History of St. Paul's Church," manuscript, St. Paul's Church, c. 1950.

Flint, William Willard, Jr., manuscript history of St. Paul's School Chapel, St. Paul's School, Concord, N.H., 1933.

Fremmer, Richard M., "Edward F. Searles, Millionaire," manuscript, Nevins Memorial Library, Methuen, Mass., 1948.

Hazlehurst, Franklin Hamilton, Jr., "An Introduction to the Architecture and Thought of Ralph Adams Cram," thesis, Princeton University, 1973.

Hubbard, John, "Sketches of business life of General Hubbard," manuscript, Joseph H. Darlington, Baltimore, n.d.

Hubbard, Thomas H., "T. H. H. by himself in 1906," manuscript, Joseph H. Darlington, Baltimore, 1906.

Mather, Samuel, "The Amasa Stone Memorial Chapel," Address at the dedication service, Case Western Reserve University, Cleveland, 1911.

Morgan, William, "The Architecture of Henry Vaughan," Ph.D. dissertation, University of Delaware, 1971.

New Hampshire Historical Records Survey of the Works Projects Administration, "Inventory of the Church Archives of New Hampshire," Manchester, 1942.

Osborne, [Rev.], "The Axe in the Hand of the Lord," address at the dedication service, Order of the Holy Cross, 1904.

Peter, Agnes, "The Bethlehem Chapel," manuscript, Washington Cathedral, 1934.

"Report of the Committee on the proposed Cathedral Building," manuscript, Washington Cathedral, 1906.

St. Peter's Church (Bennington, Vt.), Minutes of the Vestry, 1902–1909.

St. Thomas' Church (Dover, N.H.), Minutes of the Vestry, 1889–1891.

Smythe, Henry Herbert, "A History of St. Barnabas Parish," manuscript, St. Barnabas Church, Falmouth, Mass., n.d.

Tiedemann, Karl, "A Joy Forever," manuscript, Order of the Holy Cross, West Park, N.Y., 1961.

WORKS BY
HENRY VAUGHAN

Dates generally refer to beginning of construction and/or date of completion; some dates are approximate. Vaughan almost always designed the furnishings for his churches, including fonts, candelabra, and crosses, as well as pulpits, organ cases, and screens, etc. (and probably communion services and vestments). Those furnishings listed are those found in churches not built by Vaughan and the list represents probably only a small percentage of such commissions. A question mark before an entry indicates uncertainty about Vaughan's authorship. Brackets indicate construction not designed by Vaughan.

CALIFORNIA

San Francisco
[Grace Church] organ case, choir stalls (destroyed 1906)   1893

CONNECTICUT

New Haven
Christ Church   1895–1898

Morgan Memorial Cross   1909–1910

[Grove Street Cemetery] Pynchon gravestones   c. 1896

DISTRICT OF COLUMBIA

Cathedral of St. Peter and St. Paul

    Bodley & Vaughan designated architects   1906
    Bodley & Vaughan original plans   1907
    Bethlehem Chapel   1910–1912
    Bishop's House, Chapel of the Annunciation   1913–1914
    Sanctuary and choir   1915–1918

[St. John's Church] pulpit   c. 1907–1910

MAINE

Brunswick
Mary F. Searles Science Building, Bowdoin College   1894

Hubbard Grand Stand, Bowdoin College	1903
Hubbard Library, Bowdoin College	1902–1903
Newcastle	
Gladisfen (John Glidden House)	c. 1883
St. Andrew's Church	1883
Northeast Harbor	
St. Mary's-by-the-Sea Church	1902
Old Town	
St. James Church	1892–1894
Portland	
[St. Luke's Cathedral] pulpit, chancel rail	1885

MARYLAND

Baltimore	
[St. Luke's Church] rectory	1904

MASSACHUSETTS

Beverly Farms	
St. John's Church	1902
Boston	
[Church of the Advent] pulpit, Jesse window	c. 1907–1910
[Emmanuel Church] pulpit	
[Forest Hills Cemetery] Minot tomb	post-1899
[House of the Good Samaritan Chapel] font	
[Mt. Auburn Cemetery] Foote gravestones	c. 1912
[St. John the Evangelist] rood screen	1906
St. Margaret's Chapel	1882–1883
(altar and reredos done by Robert Casson according to	
Vaughan's design)	1921–1922
Bourne	
Jonathan Bourne Memorial Library	1896–1897
Cambridge	
St. Bartholomew's Church	1892
Chestnut Hill	
Church of the Redeemer	1913–1915
Victory Tower	1919–1920
Dorchester	

St. Mary's Church	1888
Falmouth	
St. Barnabas Memorial Church	1889–1890
Parish house	1890
Gardner	
St. Paul's Church	
Church, parish house, rectory designed (church never built)	1905
Parish house (used as church), (rectory built in 1930)	1908–1909
Great Barrington	
Kellogg Terrace (Searles Mansion)	
Music Room, Windsor Room, (other rooms?)	c. 1885–1886
? Coachman's house (burned 1885)	1882
? The Marigold (carriage house)	1882
Rebuilt	1897
Walls and gate tower (partially demolished)	1902
? Samuel Hopkins Memorial Parsonage	1883–1884
Searles High School	1897–1898
Groton	
First Groton chapel, Groton School (moved c. 1899; now Church of the Sacred Heart)	1887
St. John's Chapel, Groton School	1899–1900
Lawrence	
Lawrence Home for Aged People	1909–1910
Methuen	
All Saints Church (now St. Andrew's)	1904
Bridge across Spiket River	1913
Central Grammar School	1905
Emmanuel Primitive Methodist Church	1901
John Hancock Masonic Lodge (remodeling)	1897, 1916
The Hayloft (remodeling; demolished)	
Methuen Railroad Station	1905–1908
Park Lodge (remodeling)	c. 1900
Pine Lodge (Searles Castle)	
House (remodeling, enlargement)	c. 1887
Chapel (completed)	1918
Gate lodge and cottages	1900 ff.
Chime tower	c. 1892–1895
Stone chime tower	c. 1896

Walls	c. 1895
Red Tavern	1900
St. George's Ebenezer Primitive Methodist Church	1904–1905
Searles High School	1904–1905
Searles Mausoleum	1891
Serlo Organ Hall (Methuen Memorial Music Hall)	1899–1909
Stearns tomb	c. 1895
Treat Company Organ factory (remodeling)	c. 1889

New Bedford
St. Martin's Church	1891–1892
Jonathan Bourne Whaling Museum	1916

Newtonville
St. John's Church	1902

North Easton
[Unitarian Church] pulpit screen	1898

Sheffield
Christ Church	1912

Springfield
[Christ Church Cathedral] Brooks pulpit and font	1909

Swampscott
Church of the Holy Name	1893
Rectory	1907

Swansea
Christ Church	1899–1900
Frank S. Stevens Public Library	1900
Frank S. Stevens School	1908
[Frank S. Stevens tomb] bronze doors	c. 1915–1917

Worcester
C. M. Brent Memorial Cross (location unknown)	
[All Saints Church] altar and reredos	c. 1907

NEW HAMPSHIRE

Concord
St. Paul's School
Chapel of St. Peter and St. Paul	1886–1894
Lower School (demolished 1971)	1890–1892

Orphan's Home Chapel (demolished)	c. 1890
Library (project, not built)	1895
Annex to the study (burned 1962)	1898
Cloister between the chapel and the study (demolished 1919)	c. 1898
New Upper School	1902–1904
St. Timothy's Mission Church (demolished c. 1928)	1900–1901

Dover
St. Thomas's Church	1891–1892

Dublin
The Thistles (George Luther Foote house)	1888

Penacook
St. Mary's Church	1889–1890

Salem
North Salem United Methodist Church	1910–1911
[Old Meeting House] restoration	c. 1900
Stillwater Manor	1898–1905

Somersworth
[Forest Glade Cemetery] Furber Memorial Chapel	1897

Windham
Searles School	1907–1908
Stanton Harcourt (Searles Castle)	c. 1907–1915

NEW JERSEY

Bernardsville
[St. Bernard's Church] altar and reredos	post-1899

Hoboken
[Church of the Holy Innocents] Nave extension, tower, sacristy, choir room	1895
Lady chapel, altar	c. 1895

NEW YORK

New York (Manhattan)
Bourne Workshop for the Blind	1912

Cathedral of St. John the Divine	
Chapel of St. Boniface	1916
Chapel of St. James	1916
Chapel of St. Ansgar	1918
Font	c. 1915–1917
Potter Memorial Pulpit	1916

Church of the Good Shepherd	1902–1903
Arthur Brooks Memorial Parish House	1901–1902
[Church of the Incarnation] Chapel of the Nativity	1903
Holy Cross Mission Church (demolished)	1885

New York (Bronx)
Church of the Mediator	1911
Rectory designed (not built)	c. 1911

Tannersville
St. John Evangelist	c. 1884

West Park
Holy Cross Monastery	1902–1904

OHIO

Cleveland
Amasa Stone Memorial Chapel, Western Reserve University	1909–1911

PENNSYLVANIA

Philadelphia
[St. James-the-Less] organ case	c. 1907
[St. Mark's Church] Cloister, cloister doors, choir stalls, organ gallery and grille, chancel-sacristy door, rood beam and rood, rebuilding of foundations	1894–1906

RHODE ISLAND

Block Island
Dream House (Searles Mansion, burned 1963)	1886–1888

Providence
[St. Stephen's Church] rood screen, choir stalls	1883
Chancel gates	1893

VERMONT

Bennington
[St. Peter's Church] altar and reredos	1909

Lyndonville
St. Peter's Church	1898

WISCONSIN

Fond du Lac
[St. Paul's Cathedral] Grafton tomb	1913
?St. Michael's Chapel	

THE ALMIGHTY WALL

CHINA
Shanghai
? Church or school chapel   pre-1913

OTHER WORKS
Bradlee Memorial Cross (location unknown)   post-1899

INDEX

203

New Bedford, Mass., Old Dartmouth Historical Society   114, 115
New Haven, Conn., Christ Church   49, 50, 51, 55
New York, Church of the Mediator   61
New York, New-York Historical Society   74, 75
Amy Reichman   58
Shepley, Bulfinch, Richardson & Abbott   12
Margaret Stavridi   10
Swampscott, Mass., Church of the Holy Name   18, 20
Swansea, Mass., Christ Church   33
Thomas-Photos, Oxford   53, 96
Peter Vanderwarker   4, 132
E. A. Vincent   92
Elliott Viney   101
Washington, D.C., Washington Cathedral   62, 63, 64, 65, 66, 67, 68, 69,
    71, 72, 73
West Park, N.Y., Order of the Holy Cross   45, 46, 106
Williamstown, Mass., Williams College   80
Blakeslee Wright   35

All other photographs by the author

PHOTOGRAPHIC SOURCES